HARD SAY-INGS OF THE OLD TESTAMENT

Walter C. Kaiser, Jr.

Clay Knick

INTERVARSITY PRESS
DOWNERS GROVE, ILLINOIS 60515

InterVarsity Press is the book-publishing division of InterVarsity Christian Fellowship, a student movement active on campus at hundreds of universities, colleges and schools of nursing. For information about local and regional activities, write Public Relations Dept., InterVarsity Christian Fellowship, 6400 Schroeder Rd., P.O. Box 7895, Madison, WI 53707-7895.

Distributed in Canada through InterVarsity Press, 860 Denison St., Unit 3, Markham, Ontario L3R 4H1, Canada.

All Scripture quotations, unless otherwise indicated, are from the Holy Bible, New International Version. Copyright © 1973, 1978, International Bible Society. Used by permission of Zondervan Bible Publishers.

Cover illustration: Dian Ameen-Newbern

ISBN 0-8308-1221-0

Printed in the United States of America

Library of Congress Cataloging in Publication Data

Kaiser, Walter C.
    Hard sayings of the Old Testament.

    Includes index.
     1. Bible.   O.T.—Criticism, interpretation, etc.
I. Title.
BS1171.2.K26   1988   221.6   88-8836
ISBN 0-8308-1221-0

17	16	15	14	13	12	11	10	9	8	7	6	5	4	3	2	1
99	98	97	96	95	94	93	92	91	90	89	88					

Dedicated to all students of the Old Testament,
especially my brothers
and sisters and their spouses
Paul and Millie
Roger and Dottie
Ethel and Dave
Judy and Dick
Dan and Jill

Introduction

All too often people tell me they have tried to read through the Old Testament but find too much of it hard to understand. Despite their good intentions, many have abandoned the project out of sheer frustration, discouragement or puzzlement. It is not surprising that so many people find the Bible difficult, for our culture has lost contact with the Old Testament. Thus the book remains a closed document and often is treated as an artifact of our primitive origins.

Nothing, of course, could be further from the truth! The Old Testament contains some of the most fascinating and dramatic portions of the entire Bible. Furthermore, if we decide its message is irrelevant to our generation, we are misled by our own false assumptions.

Following our Lord's example, we should take up the Old Testament once again, confident that not even one passage will pass away until all have been fulfilled (Mt 5:18). In fact, the Old Testament is so relevant that our Lord warned that anyone who breaks the least Old Testament commandment, or teaches others to do so, will be called the least in the kingdom of heaven! That ought to give us pause!

Hard Sayings of the Old Testament is a response to the cries of thousands of laity (and "tell it not in Gath," clergy as well!). I have tried to answer some of the more difficult sayings which fall into

two categories: sayings for which no explanation appears to be
given and sayings which seem to contradict other portions of
Scripture.

Admittedly, the choice of these seventy-three hard sayings is
somewhat arbitrary and reflects my own experience addressing
students' questions for the past thirty years. I would enjoy hearing from readers if there are additional sayings they wish had
been included. Should this book find a happy reception among
the reading public, future editions could expand this meager beginning or see companion volumes added. But for now I believe
I have culled out the most sensitive and puzzling of all the hard
sayings of the Old Testament.

Why should we contemplate hard sayings at all? The obvious
answer is that scores of serious readers want to understand the
difficult issues in Scriptures. Besides this, by wrestling with
Scripture, we can sharpen our attention to the details in all of our
Lord's Word. Thus the more intently and patiently we examine
the text, the more handsome the dividends to our spiritual
growth.

It was the famous Bishop Whately who commented,

The seeming contradictions in scripture are too numerous not
to be the result of design; and doubtless were designed, not
as mere difficulties to try our faith and patience, but as fur-
nishing the most suitable mode of introduction that could
have been devised by mutually explaining and modifying and
limiting or extending one another's meaning. (*On Difficulties in
the Writings of St. Paul*, Essay VII, sec. 4)

He continued:

Instructions thus conveyed are evidently more striking and
more likely to arouse attention; and thus, from the very circumstance that they call for careful reflection, more likely to
make a lasting impression.

Others may debate the deliberate design of the difficulties (for often the problem results from our distance from the idiom of that day), but there can be no debate over the therapeutic effect that they produce through our increased efforts to understand and obey God's Word.

Disagreements within Scripture also supply strong incidental proof that there was no collusion among the sacred writers. The variations, instead, go a long way toward establishing the credibility both of the writers and their texts.

These hard sayings also may be viewed as a test of our commitment to Christ. Difficult passages can be handy excuses for begging off and following the Savior no longer. Our Lord spoke in parables for just this reason: So that some who thought they saw, perceived and heard would actually miss seeing, perceiving and hearing (Mk 4:12). Indeed, the apparent harshness and obscurity of some of our Lord's sayings rid him (Jn 6:66) of followers who were unwilling to be taught or were halfhearted in their search. They were not willing to look beyond the surface of the issues.

The matter remains where Butler in his famous *Analogy* left it: These hard sayings afford "opportunity to an unfair mind for explaining away and deceitfully hiding from itself that evidence which it might see" (*Analogy*, Part II, ch. vi). For those who seek an occasion to cavil at difficulties, the opportunity is hereby offered in these hard sayings.

There is nothing wrong or unspiritual, of course, about doubting—so long as one continues to search for a resolution. But there are some who, as John W. Haley put it so well,

Cherish a cavilling spirit, who are bent upon misapprehending the truth, and urging captious and frivolous objections [and who] find in the inspired volume difficulties and disagreements which would seem to have been designed as stumblingstones for those which "stumble at the word, being disobedient: whereunto also they were appointed" [1 Pet 2:8]. Upon

the wilful votaries of error God sends "strong delusion, that they should believe a lie" [2 Thess 2:11], that they might work out their own condemnation and ruin. (*An Examination of the Alleged Discrepancies of the Bible*, Andover, Mass., 1874, p. 40)
That is strong medicine for our more urbane and tame ways of disagreeing with objectors today; nevertheless, the matters Haley's quote raises are highly relevant to the discussion of hard sayings.

This work on the various discrepancies in the Old Testament stands in a long tradition of discussion on this topic. Among the early church fathers, Eusebius, Chrysostom, Augustine and Theodoret devoted whole treatises, or parts thereof, to this subject.

The subject apparently dropped out of favor from the latter part of the fifth, to the beginning of the sixteenth century A.D. There are almost no extant works that can be cited on this subject for that period of time. However, the Reformation gave a whole new impetus to the study of the Bible, as well as to this subject. John W. Haley, in his magisterial 1874 work entitled *An Examination of the Alleged Discrepancies of the Bible*, was able to cite forty-two works from the Reformation or post-Reformation era dealing with this topic (pp. 437-42).

For example, a 1527 Latin work by Andreas Althamer went through sixteen editions and dealt with some one hundred and sixty alleged discrepancies. Joannes Thaddaeus and Thomas Man put out a 1662 London publication with the title *The Reconciler of the Bible Inlarged* [sic], in which more than three thousand contradictions throughout the Old and New Testaments are fully and plainly reconciled. This work counted each discrepancy twice, for their earlier editions only had one thousand and fifty cases. Furthermore, complained Haley, he included "a multitude of trivial discrepancies, and omit[ted] many of the more important [ones]."

Oliver St. John Cooper's *Four Hundred Texts of Holy Scripture with their corresponding passages explained* included only fifty-seven instances of disagreement in this 1791 London publication.

Coming to relatively more recent times, Samuel Davidson's *Sacred Hermeneutics, Developed and Applied* included one hundred and fifteen apparent contradictions from pages 516-611 in the 1843 Edinburgh text.

The history of this discussion is filled with the names of the great biblical scholars of another day. Our generation, like theirs, must also continue to grapple with these texts for the very reasons I have already outlined.

One final note. This introduction would be incomplete if I did not express my special appreciation to my wife, Marge, for her help in bringing this book to completion. This task was undertaken in the midst of an extremely busy academic year, filled with many administrative duties, along with the two joys of my life: teaching at the seminary and speaking at conferences both in the United States and abroad. A special vote of thanks is also due to my Administrative Assistant, Mrs. Lois Armstrong, for the way she handled the duties in the Academic Dean's Office with the barest amount of direction and encouragement. It is also a pleasure to acknowledge the assistance and patience of Associate Editors Joan Lloyd Guest and James Hoover from InterVarsity Press. Their encouragement during times when this project seemed to be impossible, because of work demands, has been more than slightly responsible for its completion.

I pray that this volume may be used to create a whole new wave of enthusiasm for reading and studying the as-yet-untapped resources of the Old Testament. If it contributes to this goal by removing some of the old impediments, my efforts will have been more than worthwhile.

• CHAPTER 1 •

Fill the Earth and Subdue It

God blessed them and said to them, "Be fruitful
and increase in number; fill the earth
and subdue it. Rule over the fish of the sea
and the birds of the air and over every living
creature that moves on the ground."
GENESIS 1:28

Does the blessing pronounced by God in Genesis 1 give encouragement for us, the human race, to treat the environment in any way we choose? Is the present ecological imbalance observed in so many parts of the world the result of our orthodox Christian arrogance toward nature, as Lynn White, Jr., charged in his famous article, "The Historical Roots of Our Ecological Crisis," in *Science* (vol. 155, March 10, 1967, pp. 1203-7)?

At long last, it is generally accepted that Western scientific and technological leadership must find its roots in the biblical revelation of the reality of the visible world and the fact that the world had a beginning. (The idea of a beginning was impossible

nework of the previous cyclical notions of time.)
Judeo-Christian heritage fosters such science-ad-
ts as *uniformitarianism*, a concept that was instru-
Scientific Revolution of the seventeenth century
ial Revolution of the eighteenth century. But the
nunity has given this recent recognition very

ad this battle been won than an accompanying
eled, which is to say that the Bible taught that "it
that man exploit nature for his own proper ends"
istorical Roots," p. 1205). What we had lost, eco-
ding to Lynn White, Jr., was the spirit of pagan
says that every tree, spring, stream and hill pos-
ian spirit which had to be placated should any
ade into the environment by cutting down the
he mountain or damming the brook. Christianity
itive animism, so White argued, and made it pos-
nature with an attitude of indifference for all
. Genesis 1:28 could be cited as the Christian's
st that.

is schema is a distortion of the verse and Scripture
eed all things are equally the result of God's crea-
efore nature is real and has great worth and value.
rence between humanity and all the rest of crea-
d placed his image in men and women and thus
gave them extra value and worth and set the whole creative
order before them for their stewardship.

The gift of "dominion" over nature was not intended to be a
license to use or abuse selfishly the created order in any way men
and women saw fit. In no sense were humans to be bullies and
laws to themselves; Adam and his wife were to be responsible to
God and accountable for all the ways in which they did or did not
cultivate the natural world about them.

True, the words *subdue* and *rule over* do imply that nature will not yield easily and that some type of coercion will be necessary. Because the created order has been affected by sin just as dramatically as the first human pair were, the natural created order will not do our bidding gladly or easily. We must exert a good deal of our strength and energy into our efforts to use nature.

But such an admission does not constitute a case for the rape of the land. It is a twisted use of this authorization to perform such a task with a fierce and perverted delight. Only when our iniquities are subdued by God (Mic 7:10) are we able to exercise this function properly.

God is still the owner of the natural world (Ps 24:1), and all the beasts of the forest and the cattle on a thousand hills are his (Ps 50:10-12). Mortals are mere stewards under God. Under no condition may we abuse and run roughshod over the natural order for the sake of quick profits or for the sheer fun of doing so. Indeed, even Job was aware that the land would cry out against him if, in God's eyes, Job abused it (Job 31:38-40).

Not even in the renovation of the New Heavens and the New Earth is there a total break and a complete disregard for the present heavens and earth. Instead, the final fire of judgment will only have the effect of *purifying* because "the elements will be destroyed by fire, and the earth and everything in it will be laid bare" (2 Pet 3:5-13). Even so, the earth will not be burned up!

Lynn White felt we would be better off if we asserted, as did St. Francis of Assisi, the equality of all creatures, including human beings. This would take away from human beings any idea of a limitless rule over creation.

But such an equity fails to comprehend the concept of the image of God in persons. Trees, ants, birds and wildlife are God's creatures, but they are not endowed with his image, neither are they responsible to God for the conduct and use of the creation. What limits humanity is the fact that each must answer to God for one's use or abuse of the whole created order.

Should you ask, "What, then, happened to the cultural mandate given to the human race in Genesis?" we will respond by noting that the mandate is intact. However, it is found not here in Genesis 1:28 but rather in Genesis 2:15. There Adam is given the task to "work" the garden of Eden and to "take care of it." That is the cultural mandate.

CHAPTER 2

For When You Eat of It You Will Surely Die

*But you must not eat from the tree
of the knowledge of good and evil,
for when you eat of it you
will surely die.*
GENESIS 2:17

Clearly the penalty for disobeying God's command was death. So then, why did not Adam and Eve drop dead the same day that they disobeyed? Adam lived to be 930 years old according to Genesis 5:5. Was Satan's word in Genesis 3:4—"You will not surely die"—a more accurate assessment of the real state of affairs? What would this do to our concepts of God and Satan if Satan were more scrupulously honest than God himself?

This hard saying calls for an examination of at least three different concepts embraced within the quotation from Genesis 2:17—that is to say: (1) the tree of the knowledge of good and evil; (2) the meaning of the phrase "when [more literally, *in the day*] you eat of it"; and (3) the meaning of the phrase *you will surely die*.

First the tree. There are no grounds whatsoever for believing that the tree was a magical symbol or that it contained a secret enzyme which would automatically induce a wide body of knowledge that embraced the whole gamut of good and evil. Instead it is safer to assume that the tree was the God-appointed instrument which functioned much as the New Testament ordinance or sacrament of the Lord's Supper or Eucharist does. The tree, like the bread or the wine of the Eucharist, was indeed a real symbol embodied in an actual tree. And just as the Tree of Life was also a real tree, yet it too symbolized the fact that life was a special gift given to individuals from God. That is why participants are warned not to partake of the elements of the Lord's Supper in an unworthy manner, for when the elements are eaten and drunk in a flippant manner and when a person has not truly confessed Christ as Savior, the unworthy partaking of these rather ordinary elements (ordinary at least from all outward appearances) will cause illness and, in some cases, death (1 Cor 11:30).

In the same way, the tree was a symbol to test the first human couple's actions. Would they obey God or assert their own wills in contradistinction to God's clear command? To argue that the tree had magical power to confer knowledge of good and evil would be to miss the divine point: the tree was a test of the couple's intention to obey God. That men and women can attain the knowledge of good and evil is not in itself either undesirable or blameworthy; knowledge per se was not what was being forbidden here. The tree only represents the possibility that creatures made in God's image could refuse to obey him. The tree served as the concrete expression of that rebellion.

It is just as naive to insist that the phrase *in the day* means that on that very day death would occur. A little knowledge of the Hebrew idiom will likewise relieve the tension here as well. For example, in 1 Kings 2:37 King David warned a seditious Shimei, "The day you leave [Jerusalem] and cross the Kidron Valley [which is immediately outside the city walls on the east side of the city], you can be sure you will die." Neither the 1 Kings nor Genesis text implies *immediacy of action* on that very same day; instead, they point to the *certainty of the predicted consequence* that would be set in motion by the act initiated on that day. Alternate wordings include: *at the time when, at that time, now when* and *the day [when]* (see Gen 5:1; Ex 6:28; 10:28; 32:34).

The final concern is over the definition of death. Scripture refers to three different types of death. Often only the context helps distinguish which is intended. There are physical death, spiritual death (the kind that forces guilty persons to hide from the presence of God, as this couple did when it was time for fellowship in the Garden, in Gen 3:8), and the "second death" (which Revelation 20:14 refers to when a person is finally, totally and eternally separated from God without hope of reversal, after a lifetime of rejecting God).

In this case, spiritual death was the immediate outcome of disobedience demonstrated by a deliberate snatching of real fruit from a real tree in a real garden. Death ensued immediately: They became "dead . . . in transgressions and sins" (Eph 2:1-3). But such separation and isolation from God eventually resulted in physical death as well. This, however, was more a by-product than a direct result of their sin. Spiritual death was the real killer!

· C H A P T E R 3 ·

I Will Make a Helper Suitable for Him

The LORD God said, "It is not good for man to be alone. I will make a helper suitable for him."
GENESIS 2:18

Are women inferior to men, merely designed to be their helpers? Would we be more consistent with the biblical text if we viewed men as the initiators and women as assistants to men? Is this what makes women suitable matches for men?

The Creator regarded Adam's situation as incomplete and deficient while he was living without community or a proper counterpart. The Creator judged Adam's situation quite negatively: "It is not good."

Ecclesiastes 4:9-12 expresses this same opinion about aloneness. The wise writer Solomon advised:

Two are better than one. . . . If one falls down, his friend can

help him up. . . . Also, if two lie down together, they will keep
warm. But how can one keep warm alone? Though one may
be overpowered, two can defend themselves.

True, the prophet Jeremiah is commanded by God to remain
alone in Jeremiah 16:1-9, but this is meant to be a sign that God's
judgment on the people is so near that it will not be worthwhile
to try getting married. Nevertheless, the full life is a life that
finds its fulfillment in community with another person or group
of persons.

In the Genesis story we find that God created a woman after
he had created the man. This would end Adam's loneliness and
the state which God judged to be "not good" and negative. She
was to be his "helper"—at least that is how most of the translations have interpreted this word from Genesis 2:18. A sample
of the translations read as follows: "I shall make a helper fit for
him" (Revised Standard Version); "I will make a fitting helper for
him" (New Jewish Publication Society); "I will make an aid fit for
him" (Anchor Bible); "I will make him a helpmate" (Jerusalem
Bible); "I will make a suitable partner for him" (New American
Bible); "I will make him a helper comparable to him" (New King
James Version).

However, the customary translation of the two words *'ezer
kenegdo* as "helper fitting him" is almost certainly wrong. Recently
R. David Freedman has pointed out that the Hebrew word *'ezer*
is a combination of two roots: *'-z-r* meaning "to rescue, to save"
and *ǵ-z-r* meaning "to be strong." The difference between the two
is the first sign in Hebrew. Today that letter is silent in Hebrew,
but in ancient times it was a guttural sound formed in the back
of the throat. The *g* was a *ghayyin*, and like the other sign *'ayin*,
both came to use the same symbol in the Hebrew alphabet. But
the fact that they were pronounced differently is clear from such
place names which preserve the *g* sound such as *Gaza* or *Gomorrah*. Some Semitic languages distinguished between these two

signs and others did not; for example, Ugaritic did make a distinction between the *'ayin* and the *ghayyin;* Hebrew did not (R. David Freedman, "Woman, A Power Equal to a Man," *Biblical Archaeology Review* 9 [1983]:56-58).

It would appear that sometime around 1500 B.C. these two signs began to be represented by one sign in Phoenician. Consequently the two phonemes merged into one grapheme and what had been two different roots merged into one, much as in English the one word *fast* can refer to a person's speed, his observing "a fast," his or her slyness in a "fast deal" or the adamant way in which she or he held "fast" to positions. The noun *'ezer* occurs twenty-one times in the Old Testament. In many of the passages, it is used in parallelism to words which clearly denote strength or power. Some examples are:

There is none like the God of Jeshurun, The Rider of the Heavens in your strength *('-z-r)*, and on the clouds in his majesty. (Deut 33:26, my translation)

Blessed are you, O Israel! Who is like you, a people saved by the Lord? He is the shield of your strength *('-z-r)* and the sword of your majesty. (Deut 33:29, my translation)

The case that begins to build is that we can be sure that *'ezer* means "strength" or "power" whenever it is used in parallelism with words for majesty or other words for power such as *'oz* or *'uzzo.* In fact, the presence of two names for one king, Azariah and Uzziah (both referring to God's strength), makes it abundantly clear that the root *'ezer* meaning "strength" was known in Hebrew.

Therefore I suggest that we translate Genesis 2:18 as "I will make a power [or strength] corresponding to man." Freedman even suggests on the basis of later Hebrew that the second word in the Hebrew expression found in this verse should be rendered *equal to him.* If this is so, then God makes for the man a woman fully his equal and fully his match. In this way, the man's loneliness will be assuaged.

The same line of reasoning occurs in the apostle Paul. He urged in 1 Corinthians 11:10, "For this reason, a woman must have power [or authority] on her head" [that is to say invested in her].

This line of reasoning which stresses full equality is continued in Genesis 2:23 where Adam says of Eve: "This is now bone of my bones and flesh of my flesh; she shall be called 'woman,' for she was taken out of man." The idiomatic sense of this phrase *bone of my bones* is a "very close relative," "one of us" or in effect "our equal."

The woman was never meant to be an assistant or "helpmate" to the man. The word *mate* slipped into English since it was so close to Old English *meet*, which means "fit to" or "corresponding to" the man. That all comes from the phrase I have suggested likely means "equal to."

What God had intended then was to make a "power" or "strength" for the man who would in every way "correspond to him" or even "be his equal."

· C H A P T E R 4 ·

God Knows You Will Be Like God

---

*For God knows that when you eat of
it your eyes will be opened, and
you will be like God, knowing
good and evil.*
GENESIS 3:5

Can the wisdom of mortals equal God's? Again we must ask if the
Serpent was more honest with Adam and Eve than God was. The
Serpent had explained God's prohibition against eating from the
fruit of these trees from the motive of divine envy "lest [the man
and woman] become like one of us!" But what wisdom, then, did
the man and woman attain?

Some have seen parallels in this passage to the Babylonian
flood story, called the Gilgamesh Epic, in which the wild man
Enkidu, who is finally civilized by spending six days and seven
nights with a prostitute, sees the animals flee from him, and the
woman congratulates him: "You are wise, Enkidu. You have be-

come as a god." But the two sentences from Genesis 3:15 and Gilgamish are totally different, and Enkidu sheds no light on our passage, contrary to undemonstrated assurances from a number of leading scholars.

There are five passages in which the antithetical pair, *good* and *evil*, and the verb *to know* occur: Deuteronomy 1:39; 2 Samuel 14:17; 19:35; 1 Kings 3:9; and Isaiah 7:15. These passages help to dismiss certain theories that have been proposed. Certainly we cannot say that Adam and Eve attained premature sexual union due to the aphrodisiac qualities of the fruit on these trees. The only argument in favor of this dubious sexual interpretation is the awakening of shame (Gen 3:7) and the punishment on the woman which was placed in what some construe as the area of her sexuality (Gen 3:16). However, even while the disturbance affected the sexual aspect of personhood, the text makes it clear that the knowledge of good and evil is a divine prerogative (Gen 3:5, 22). The extension of a sexual interpretation to God is obviously grotesque and unwarranted.

This would mean that man could become like God either by attaining total knowledge, or as we shall argue, by having autonomy, particularly moral freedom. Such wisdom "to know good and evil" can be seen in 2 Samuel 19:35 where Barzillai as an eighty-year-old man doubts his ability to exhibit such knowledge between good and evil needed from the king's counselor. Likewise, the woman from Tekoa likened David to an angel who was able to discern good and evil (2 Sam 14:17). Solomon asked that God would also give him "a discerning heart to govern your people and to distinguish between right and wrong" (1 Kings 3:9).

The lure of the Serpent, then, did not imply that humanity would have infinite knowledge like God's knowledge or even that there was some aphrodisiac in the fruit which would open up sexual or carnal relations as an option until then unknown. Instead, the lure of the Serpent was an invitation to experience that perpetual quest of human autonomy and freedom. Unfortunately for all, that autonomy turned out to be illusory and actually ended up in a sense of alienation, which has been studied so often since Freud introduced the concept to the modern world.

· C H A P T E R   5 ·

I Will Greatly Increase Your Pains

*To the woman he said, . . . I will
greatly increase your pains in
childbearing; with pain you
will give birth to children.*
GENESIS 3:16

If *bearing children was declared a blessing from God in Genesis 1:28,*
why did God totally reverse this blessing as a result of the Fall?
Indeed, the word *pains,* which reappears in verse 17 in the curse
on man as well, is said to have increased. But no pain had been
mentioned previously; only a blessing.

There is no doubt that this term refers to physical pain. Its root
lies in a verb that means "to injure, cause pain or grieve." Whether the pain would lie in the agony of childbirth or in the related
grief that accompanies raising that child cannot be finally determined; the text would seem to allow for both ideas.

Katherine C. Bushnell, in her famous work *God's Word to Wom-*

an, suggests that verse 16 be translated differently since the Hebrew text could support such a reading. She noted that some ancient versions attached the meaning of "lying in wait," or "an ambush," or "a snare," to the word generally read as *multiply.* This idea of a snare or a lying in wait, however, may have been moved back to verse 15 from its more normal position of verse 16. Bushnell would render the opening words of verse 16 this way: "Unto the woman he said, 'A snare has increased your sorrow and sighing.' "

This translation is not all that different from the more traditional, "I will greatly multiply . . ." The difference between the two readings is found wholly in the interlinear Hebrew vowel signs which came as late as the eighth century of the Christian era. The difference is this (using capital letters to show the original Hebrew consonantal text and lowercase to show the late addition of the vowel letters): *HaRBah AaRBeh,* "I will greatly multiply" and *HiRBah AoReB,* "has caused to multiply (or made great) a lying-in-wait." The participial form *ARB appears some fourteen times in Joshua and is translated as ambush,* or *a lying in wait.*

If this new reading is correct (and some ancient versions read such a word just a few words back in verse 15, probably by misplacement), then that "lier-in-wait" would undoubtedly be that subtle serpent, the devil. He it was who would increase the sorrow of raising children. This is the only way we can explain why the idea of "a snare" or "lying-in-wait" still clings to this context.

But another matter demands our attention in verse 16, the word for *conception.* This translation is difficult because the Hebrew word *HRN* is not the correct way to spell *conception.* It is spelled correctly as *HRJWN* in Ruth 4:13 and Hosea 9:11 when it meant *conception.* But this spelling in Genesis 3:16 is two letters short and is regarded by the lexical authorities such as Brown, Driver and Briggs as a contraction or even an error.

All Hebrew authorities acknowledge that not only are some
consonantal letters missing for the meaning of *conception*, but the
vowels are also unusual. The early Greek translation (made in
the third or second century before Christ) read instead *HGN*,
meaning "sighing." The resultant meaning for this clause would
be, "A snare has increased your sorrow and sighing."

What difference does such a rendering make, you ask? The
point is simply that this curse cannot be read to mean that the
right to determine when a woman will become a mother is placed
totally outside her will or that this function has been placed
entirely and necessarily in the hands and will of her husband.

Futhermore, it must be remembered that this statement, no
matter how we shall finally interpret it, is from a curse passage.
In no case should it be made normative. And if the Evil One and
not God is the source of the sorrow and sighing, then it is all the
more necessary for us to refuse to place any degree of normativity to such statements and describe either the ordeal of giving
birth to a child, or the challenge of raising that child, as an evil
originating in God. God is never the source of evil; he would
rather bless women. Instead, it is Satan who has set this trap.

The next clause strengthens the one we have been discussing
by adding, "in sorrow (or *pain*) you will bring forth children."
Once again note that bearing children in itself was a blessing
described in the so-called orders of creation of Genesis 1:28. The
grief lies not so much in the conception or in the act of childbirth
itself, but in the whole process of bringing children into the
world and raising them up to be whole persons before God.

• CHAPTER 6 •

Your Desire Will Be for Your Husband

*To the woman he said, . . . "Your
desire will be for your husband,
and he will rule over you."*
GENESIS 3:16

The second part of the woman's penalty centers around the translation
of two very important words which have a most amazing history
of translation: "desire" and "shall rule." Seldom has so much
mischief been caused by the history of a translation error which
became institutionalized.

Is it true that due to the Fall women naturally exhibit over-
powering sexual desires for their husbands? And if this is so, did
God simultaneously order the husbands to exercise authority
over their wives? In one form or another, most conservative
interpreters answer both of these questions emphatically yes and
point to Genesis 3:16 as the grounds for their answer. But will

the text itself bear the weight of such important claims?

The Hebrew word *teshuqah*, now almost universally translated as "desire," was previously rendered as "turning." The word only appears in the Hebrew Old Testament three times: Here in Genesis 3:16, in Genesis 4:7 and in Song of Solomon 7:10. Of the twelve known ancient versions (the Greek Septuagint, the Syriac Peshitta, the Samaritan Pentateuch, the Old Latin, the Sahidic, the Bohairic, the Ethiopic, the Arabic, Aquila's Greek, Symmachus's Greek, Theodotion's Greek and the Latin Vulgate), almost every one (twenty-one out of twenty-eight times) renders these three instances of *teshuqah* as "turning," not "desire."

Likewise, the Church Fathers (Clement of Rome, Irenaeus, Tertullian, Origen, Epiphanius and Jerome, along with Philo, a Jew who died about A.D. 50) seem to be ignorant of any other sense for this word *teshuqah* than the translation of "turning." Furthermore, the Latin rendering was *conversio* and the Greek was *apostrophe* or *epistrophe*, words all meaning a "turning."

With such strong and universal testimony in favor of "turning," how did the idea of desire ever intrude into the translator's agenda? Again, it was Katherine C. Bushnell who did the pioneer research on this problem. She traced its genesis to an Italian Dominican monk named Pagnino who translated the Hebrew Bible. Pagnino, according to the infamous biblical critic Richard Simon, "too much neglected the ancient versions of Scripture to attach himself to the teachings of the rabbis." Pagnino's version was published in Lyons in 1528, seven years before Coverdale's English Bible. Now except for Wycliffe's 1380 English version and the Douay Bible of 1609, both of which were made from the Latin Vulgate, every English version from the time of Pagnino up to the present day has adopted Pagnino's rendering for Genesis 3:16.

The older English Bibles, following Pagnino, rendered our verse as follows: "Thy lust [or lusts] shall pertayne [pertain] to

thy husband." Clearly, then, the sense given to the word by
Pagnino and his followers was that of libido or sensual desire.
The only place that Bushnell could locate such a concept was in
the "Ten Curses of Eve" in the Talmud.

It is time the church returned to the real meaning of this word.
The sense of Genesis 3:16 is simply this: As a result of her sin,
Eve would turn away from her sole dependence on God and turn
now to her husband. The results would not at all be pleasant,
warned God, as he announced this curse.

Nowhere does this text teach, nor does nature confirm by our
observations, that there would now be a tendency for a woman
to be driven by a desire for sexual relationships with her husband
or with other men. This is both a misrepresentation of the text
and a male fantasy born out of some other source than from the
Bible or human nature. Even if the word is tamed down to mean
just an inclination or a tendency, we would be no further ahead.
These renderings would still miss the point of the Hebrew. The
Hebrew reads: "You are turning away [from God!] to your husband, and [as a result] he will rule over you [take advantage of
you]."

Though this text only predicts how some husbands will take
advantage of their wives, when the wives turn to their husbands
after turning away from God, some argue that this second verb
should be rendered "he shall rule over you." This would make the
statement mandatory with the force of a command addressed to
all husbands to rule over their wives.

The Hebrew grammar once again will not allow this construction. The verb contains a simple statement of futurity; there is
not one hint of obligation or normativity in this verb. To argue
differently would be as logical as demanding that a verb in verse
18 be rendered, "It *shall produce* thorns and thistles." Thereafter,
all Christian farmers who used weed killer would be condemned
as disobedient to the God who demanded that the ground have

such thorns and thistles.

The often-repeated rejoinder to this *will rule/shall rule* argument is to go to Genesis 4:7: "Sin is crouching at the door; unto
you is its turning, but you will [or *shall* in the sense of *must*] rule
over it." There is no doubt that both the word *teshuqah* ("turning")
and the verb *to rule* are found in both contexts. But what is
debated is the best way to render the Hebrew.

Several suggestions avoid the traditional interpretation which
insists on an obligatory sense to the verb *to rule*. One way predicts
that Cain, now governed by sin and pictured as a crouching beast
at his door, will rule over him (his brother, Abel). This, however,
does not appear to be what the author meant.

A preferred way of handling this phrase would be to treat it
as a question. (The absence of the particle introducing questions
is a phenomenon witnessed in about half of Hebrew questions).
Hence, we would render it, "But you, will you rule over it?" or
"Will you be its master?" (This interpretation is also favored by
H. Ewald, G. R. Castellino and, to some extent, Claus Wester-
mann).

Even though many hold to the belief that 1 Corinthians 14:34
refers to Genesis 3:16 when it records: "Women should remain
silent in the churches. They are not allowed to speak, but must
be in submission, as the Law says," I cannot agree. When the
Corinthians referred to the Law (it seems that Paul is answering
a previous question they wrote to him) it was to the Jewish law
found in the Talmud and Mishnah that they referred. There it
was taught that a woman should not speak and that she must
be silent, but that is not taught in the Old Testament!

The only conceivable way a person could link up Genesis 3:16
with 1 Corinthians 14:34-35 would be if the Genesis passage said
husbands must rule over their wives. Since such wording of the
verse has been proven impossible, this reference must be graciously surrendered. We should lay no stronger burden on God's

people than what is warranted in God's Word.

Later on in God's revelation, our Lord will affirm a job sub-ordination within the marriage relationship, and the husband will be answerable to God for the well-being of his wife and family. However, Genesis 3:16 does not carry any of those meanings.

We may conclude, then, that *teshuqah* does not refer to the lust or sexual appetite of a woman for a man. Neither does the verb *to rule* over her express God's order for husbands in their relationships to their wives.

· C H A P T E R 7 ·

Cain Lay
with
His Wife

Cain lay with his wife, and she
became pregnant.
GENESIS 4:17

Immediately *we want to know, where did Cain get his wife? Up to this* point we only know about Cain and Abel. This question has been asked so many times that it no doubt deserves a place in the Biblical Hall of Famous Questions.

The most obvious answer must be that Adam and Eve had other children than those explicitly mentioned thus far, including daughters. Indeed, Genesis 5:4 plainly says as much, "[Adam] had other sons and daughters."

The point is that Cain must have married his sister. But to admit this is to raise a further difficulty. Was he guilty of incest if he married his own sister?

At least two things can be said in response to this reproach. First, if the human race was propagated from a single pair, as we believe the evidence indicates, such closely related marriages were unavoidable. The demand for some other way of getting the race started is an unfair expectation.

In the second place, the notion of incest must be probed more closely. At first the sin of incest was connected with sexual relationships between parents and children. Only afterwards was the notion of incest extended to sibling relationships.

By Moses' time there were laws governing all forms of incest (Lev 18:7-17; 20:11-12, 14, 17, 20-21; Deut 22:30; 27:20, 22, 23). These laws clearly state that sexual relations or marriage is forbidden with a mother, father, stepmother, sister, brother, half-brother, granddaughter, daughter-in-law, son-in-law, aunt, uncle or brother's wife.

The Bible, in the meantime, notes that Abraham married his half-sister (Gen 20:12). Therefore, the phenomenon is not unknown in Scripture. Prior to Moses' time, incest in many of the forms later proscribed were not thought to be wrong. Thus, even Moses' own father, Amram, married a young aunt, his father's sister, Jochabed (Ex 6:20). In Egypt, the routine marriage of brothers and sisters among the Pharaohs all the way up to the second century made the Mosaic law all the more a radical break with their Egyptian past.

The genetic reasons for forbidding incest were not always an issue. Close inbreeding in ancient times was without serious or any genetic damage. Today, the risk of genetic damage is extremely high. Since the genetic possibilities of Adam and Eve were very good, there were no biological reasons for restricting marriages to the degree that it became necessary to do so later.

· CHAPTER 8 ·

Whoever Sheds the Blood of Man, by Man Shall His Blood Be Shed

Whoever sheds the blood of man, by man
shall his blood be shed: for in
the image of God has God made man.
GENESIS 9:6

Can *Genesis 9:6 properly be used to answer our modern questions* about capital punishment? The debate is one of no small proportions, and the consequences both for the condemned murderer and for society are great indeed.

Genesis 9:5-6 is the simplest statement mandating society to punish their fellow beings for murder. However, its very simplicity and lack of any development allow opponents of capital punishment to question the passage's relevancy. Missing, they claim, are all references to civil government, due process, exceptions and distinctions between various degrees of murder.

Genesis 9:5-6 is part of the covenant God established with

Noah following the flood. Involved in this covenant were the animals' fear for all persons, permission to eat meat that did not contain the lifeblood and the delegation of the death penalty for murder into the hands of men and women. But more than this was involved, and this tends to demonstrate the enduring nature of the provisions of this covenant. Seasons were instituted as part of the enduring natural order (Gen 8:22), the rainbow would serve as a continuing pledge that the earth would not be flooded again (9:13) and the image of God provided the rationale for exacting the extreme penalty (9:6). The covenant established with Noah is therefore one that involves his representing "every living creature" (Gen 6:18-19; 9:10-11, 12, 15-17).

The text has a clear statement on capital punishment. God requires a "reckoning" of both the person and beast who shed anyone's blood. But since both are held responsible, even though the beasts cannot make moral discriminations or act intentionally, how can advocates of capital punishment, such as me, use this text to sort out the issue?

We could argue that Exodus 21:28-36 supplies the principle of animal liability while the Mosaic law makes a distinction between manslaughter and murder or between first, second and third degree murder. Opponents would contend, however, that the Mosaic law was made between God and Israel while the Noahic covenant was between God and every living creature.

This distinction, however, is most curious because it makes a sharper dichotomy between law and grace than what Scripture intends. For even when the civil code of the Mosaic law demonstrates a particularistic and distinctively cultural relevancy, which is limited to the period for which they were written, these same laws have behind them eternal principles as enduring as the character of God. That is the point so clearly made by the recent discovery that the Ten Commandments, with their moral code, set the agenda for both the Covenant Code of Exodus 21—23 and the specifications of Deuteronomy 6—26. I have argued this case in some detail in my 1983 book entitled *Toward Old Testament Ethics*.

But let us settle the matter on the textual grounds of Genesis 9:6 itself. First, it is clear that the text is giving us a command and not just a suggestion or permission. Verse 5 states that God demands a punishment, "I [God] will demand an accounting for the life of his fellow man." Moreover, the reason given for this action is one that remains in force for as long as men and women are made in the image of God (v. 6).

This matter of the image of God brings us to the heart of the issue: "for [because] in the image of God has God made man." The word *for* cannot be rendered "although" here, as in Genesis 8:21 or Joshua 17:13—as if the fact that a person was made in the image of God was no impediment to the sentence of death. The clearest reading is that the murderer had to suffer for his or her actions because it was a fundamental denial of the image of God in the harmed individual. The person who destroyed another being made in God's image in fact did violence to God himself—so sacred and so permanent was the worth and value that God had invested in the slain victim.

Some interpreters connect the causal conjunction not with the shedding of blood, but with everything that preceded it—verses 1, 2 and 7. On these grounds, the reason given in the last part of verse 6 is instead the reason that God saved a remnant of the human race through Noah and why he protects people from the threats of wild animals.

But all of this is too distantly related. Furthermore, it is based on the alleged excuse that verse 6 has a peculiar structure. This seems more like special pleading than solid exegesis. Ordinarily, one takes the nearest expression when seeking the expression or word that the *for* or *because* clause modifies. More indicators are needed that claim that a chiastic word order is unusual in this situation. This happens in poetry regularly.

Others object to transferring this demand for capital punishment in verse 6 to the law books as a universally binding law without including verses 4 and 5—"You shall not eat meat that still has its lifeblood" and "I will demand an accounting from every animal." This can be partially answered by recognizing that the New Testament forbids Gentiles from eating blood or things that have not been properly bled (Acts 15:20, 29; compare with Lev 3:17; 17:14; Deut 12:16, 23). And Exodus 21:28-36 does enforce the principle of animal liability.

It is likewise too much to assert that "the shedding of blood" be taken merely as a metaphor for death. Most frequently the concept of pouring was a physical act; its metaphoric usages were reserved for such ideas as the pouring out of the wrath of God or the pouring out of one's heart or soul. But when blood was poured out in a violent way, that outpouring was said to pollute the land (Num 35:33; Deut 21:7; 2 Kings 24:4; Is 59:7; Ezek 22:3; Zeph 1:17). It is this pouring out of blood that constitutes the single most frequent use of this verb. It is hardly a metaphoric usage. No picture of violent death could be more graphically depicted.

Later in the sixth commandment, the one word is chosen to depict first degree murder out of the seven possible verbs in Hebrew for *kill*. *Rasach* became restricted to deliberate and premeditated murder (Ps 94:6; Prov 22:13; Is 1:21; Jer 7:9; Hos 4:2; 6:9). This verb was not used for killing beasts for food (Gen 9:3), defending oneself in a nighttime attack (Ex 22:2), accidental killings (Deut 19:5) or even manslaughter (Num 35:16, 25). What joins murder with manslaughter is that both incur blood guilt and both pollute the land. What differentiates the two is that there is no substitute allowed for death which comes by the hand of a murderer (that is to say, for one who premeditates his act), but the text implies that for every other of the sixteen to twenty death penalty crimes in the Old Testament, a substitute is permitted (Num 35:31). It is with this concept that the shedding of blood would appear to be linked.

Nowhere does the text introduce the political state as the one that demands that life from the murderer. While this is true, it is only another evidence of the phenomenon of progressive revelation. No one passage supplies all the details. Even the statement in Romans 13 on the state does not include the caveat raised in Acts 4:19-20 which circumscribes the authority of the state over a Christian when obeying human government would exclude obeying God.

Jesus himself seems to have accepted the principle of capital punishment when he reminded Pilate that government was divinely conferred (Jn 19:11). The same position is elsewhere supported in the New Testament by Romans 13:4 and Acts 25:11. However, the major argument for capital punishment still rests in the image-of-God argument given in Genesis 9:6. This can hardly be bypassed by any who take Scripture seriously.

But if a society persists in refusing to take the life of those conclusively proven deliberate and violent abusers of others' lives, then that society will stand under God's judgment and the value of worth, dignity and respect for persons in that society and nation will diminish accordingly. It is self-defeating to argue on the one hand for civil and female rights and to turn around on the other and deny them to the one struck down by a murderous blow.

Of course this principle must be applied with such reluctance that where "reasonable doubt" exists, we err on the side of mercy and waive the death penalty. In an imperfect judicial system not all defendants will be treated equally or fairly because economic status, social standing, race or political and legal connections will place some "above the law." However we will warn that such cheating does not escape God's notice nor does it change his laws.

It only becomes another divine indictment on that society that dares to exercise unevenly the divinely ordained demand for justice. That nation is going to be judged for such a cavalier attitude toward God's mission.

CHAPTER 9

Blessed Be Abram by God Most High

*Then Melchizedek king of Salem brought out bread
and wine. He was priest of God Most
High, and he blessed Abram, saying, "Blessed
be Abram by God Most High, Creator of
heaven and earth."*
GENESIS 14:18-19

The striking aspect of this hard saying is that the one who makes the statement is himself a Canaanite. Moreover, he is called a "priest of God Most High." In addition to his office of priest, he also is described as the king of Salem, apparently a reference to the shortened name for Jerusalem which at that time was occupied by the Canaanites.

This Gentile, about whom we have had no advance notice, either in the text or anywhere else for that matter, now comes forward to pay homage to Abram. He brings with him bread and wine as he goes out to meet Abram on his return from the amazing victory by the 318 servants of the patriarch over four

Mesopotamian kings. In so doing, the priest-king pays respect to Abram, yet he acknowledges that what has been accomplished could only be attributed to God Most High.

This is a most unexpected turn of events, for out of the grossly pagan world of the Canaanites emerges not only one who shares belief and worship in the same God as the Semitic Abram but one who pronounces the blessing on the patriarch whom God had already blessed. Abram also acknowledges the priestly dignity of this Canaanite priest-king by giving him a tithe.

This situation is very similar to that of Jethro in Exodus 18. He too was a priest who worshiped the same God Moses did, yet he too was a gentile Midianite (Ex 2:16; 3:1; 18:12). Evidently, God was also calling out a people for his own name from among the Gentiles even though the text rarely paused in its pursuit of the promise-plan of God through the Hebrew people to reflect on this phenomenon.

Who then was Melchizedek? Was he an early preincarnate appearance of Christ or, as theologians label this type of happening, a Christophony? Or was he a type of Christ, since Psalm 110:4 and Hebrews 6:20—7:21 link Christ's priesthood not to Aaron, and the famous Levitical priestly line in Israel, but with Melchizedek?

The sudden and almost mysterious appearance of Melchizedek is what gives to him that quality of timelessness and uniqueness. There can be little doubt that the text treats him as if he were a real historical character who touched the life of the biblical patriarch at a very crucial time in his service for God.

But Melchizedek also has a typological aspect to his character, not in all aspects of his person and character, but most significantly in the fact that we know absolutely nothing about his parentage or his age. This fact sets him apart from all other priests we are told about in the biblical narrative. Thus the author of Hebrews likens Melchizedek to Jesus: "Without father or mother, without genealogy, without beginning of days or end of life, like the Son of God he remains a priest forever" (Heb 7:3).

What is intended, of course, is that the biblical record does not mention Melchizedek's parents, his ancestry, his birth or his death. In that sense, he was different from any other individual found in the biblical narrative. This fact uniquely fits him to be a type of Christ. As such, he functions as a symbol of eternity. His unique priesthood offers a picture of the eternal and universal priesthood of Jesus Christ.

This explains how the Messiah could come from the promise line of Abram and eventually from the tribe of Judah and could also be a priest as well as a prophet and a king. Messiah could not come from two tribes at once, both Judah (as king) and from Levi (as priest). But he solved the dilemma by becoming a priest "not on the basis of a regulation as to his ancestry [that is, a legal requirement concerning bodily descent] but on the basis of the power of an indestructible life" (Heb 7:16).

One more point needs to be made: Abram gave a tenth to this priest-king; not the other way around. The "everything" of which Abram gave a tithe were the spoils Abram had taken in battle. This was Abram's response to Melchizedek's offer of bread and wine and the blessing which Melchizedek had offered—a blessing which normally comes from the greater person to the lesser. Strangely enough, as the author of Hebrews points out (Heb 7:10), in this sense Levi paid tithes and recognized a priesthood which would supersede his own line even before he was born, because "Levi was still in the body of his ancestor" when Abram offered the tithe to Melchizedek.

· C H A P T E R   1 0 ·

God
Tested
Abraham

Some time later God tested Abraham.
GENESIS 22:1

Even though the writer carefully couches his description of God's command to Abraham as a "test," many people have nevertheless puzzled over God's being involved in what many view as entrapment. How then shall we view this test from God?

The term used here for "to test" is used in eight other Old Testament passages where God is said to be the "tester." In six of these (Ex 15:22-26; 16:4; 20:18-20; Deut 8:2, 16; Judg 2:21-22; 3:1-4), Israel is tested. In 2 Chronicles 32:31, King Hezekiah was tested and in Psalm 26:2, David appealed to God to test him. In five of the six cases where Israel was tested, the context shows the testing stemmed from concern over the nation's obedience to

God's commands, laws or ways. That same concern is implied in
Exodus 20:18-20 where the issue is the fear of the Lord, just as
it is here in Genesis 22:1, 12. Likewise, the passages in Psalm 26
and 2 Chronicles 32:31 focus on the matter of obedience and
invite God to prove whether David and Hezekiah are not willing
to obey God with all their hearts and souls.

Therefore, based on these eight passages where God is the
subject and author of the testing, we may conclude that God
wanted to test Abraham to know his heart and to see if he would
obey and fear the Lord who gave him the son he loved so dearly.
Just as the Queen of Sheba came to "test" Solomon's wisdom (1
Kings 10:1), so God also tests without any sinister connotations.

When the word to "test" is used as a term in which man tests
or tries God, the meaning is altogether different (Ex 17:2, 7;
Num 14:22; Is 7:12). Such a test flows from an attitude of doubt
and a sinful heart on man's part. In this situation, man wants to
determine whether God's power will be adequate, the effect of
which is to "tempt" God.

But when used of God, there is no connotation of doubt or a
desire to trick or deceive the one placed under the test. His testing was only concerned with obedience or with the fear of God,
that is to say, an attitude which expressed that same spirit of
obedience to God. Deuteronomy 8:2 describes the wilderness
wanderings with its particularly harsh experiences along the way
as a testing by God—"Remember how the LORD your God led
you . . . in the desert these forty years, to humble you and to test
you in order to know what was in your heart."

Such a test demonstrated in action what Abraham claimed: he
was willing to trust the God who had provided this son born so
late in the patriarch's life.

The old English word for *test* was *to prove*. In our context it does
not have the sense of exciting to sin or provoking someone to
commit an evil. Indeed, James 1:13 states, "God cannot be tempt-

ed by evil, nor does he tempt anyone." Temptation or testing in the bad sense always proceeds from the malice of Satan working on the corruptions of our own hearts. God, however, may bring his creatures into circumstances of special testing, not for the purpose of supplying information for himself, but in order to manifest to individuals and others the dispositions of their hearts. In this context, all forms of divine testing, putting to the proof and trying individuals are used in such a way as to leave God's attributes unimpeachable.

But if it is asked, "How could a holy God put his servant through such an ordeal as this?" the answer rests in the special relationship that Abraham and the Lord enjoyed. The relationship of father and son which existed between Abraham and Isaac was exactly the same relationship which existed between God and Abraham. Abraham's test was indeed a qualifying test which had as much evidential value for Abraham as it had for the Lord who issued the test.

The point is that the test was not a temptation to do evil or a test which was meant to trap the hapless patriarch. Instead, it had the opposite purpose: it was intended to strengthen him and to build him up, as did the numerous tests in the desert. As used here, the ideas of tempting, testing or trying are religious concepts. It is God's testing the partner of the covenant to see if he is keeping his side of the agreement. God never tests the heathen; he tests his own people exclusively. Thus the test is ever a test of God's own in order to know whether they will love, fear, obey, worship and serve him.

Testing, finally, is one of the means by which God carries out his saving purposes. Often people do not know why they were tested until after the test is over. Only after they have been preserved, proved, purified, disciplined and taught can they move beyond the situation, strong in faith and strengthened for the more difficult tasks ahead.

· CHAPTER 11 ·

Sacrifice Your Son as a Burnt Offering

Then God said, "Take your son, your only son,
Isaac, whom you love, and go to the region
of Moriah. Sacrifice him there as a burnt
offering on one of the mountains that
I will tell you about."
GENESIS 22:2

What can be said of such an astonishing demand? Does God really
demand or even approve of human sacrifice?

This chapter has been unfairly linked recently with the same
kind of blind obedience operative in the tragedy at Jonestown,
Guyana. But God did not command Abraham to commit murder.
This incident is not to be classed with the foolish sacrifice of
Jepthah's daughter (Judg 11:30-40); Gibeon's demands (2 Sam
21:8, 9, 14); or the practices of Ahaz, Manasseh or Hezekiah (2
Kings 16:3; 21:6, 2 Chron 33:6). It was this practice of human
sacrifice that Josiah abolished (2 Kings 23:10) and the prophets
condemned (Jer 19:5; Ezek 20:30-31; 23:36-39). Indeed, the law

clearly prohibited the sacrifice of individuals and spoke scornfully of those who offered to Molech (Lev 18:21; 20:2) their eldest sons as human sacrifices.

In the abstract, human sacrifice cannot be condemned on principle. The truth is that God owns all life and has a right to give or take it as he wills. To reject on all grounds the right and legitimacy of our Lord to ask for life under any conditions would be to remove his sovereignty and question his justice in providing his own sacrifice as the central work of redemption.

However, our God has chosen to prohibit human sacrifice. It is this dilemma of the forthrightness of the command to Abraham versus the clear prohibition against human sacrifice which must be solved. From the chapter, it seems clear that God never intended that this command be executed. The proof for this position is that God restrained Abraham's hand just as he was about to take his son's life. " 'Do not lay a hand on the boy,' he said. 'Do not do anything to him. Now I know that you fear God, because you have not withheld from me your son, your only son' " (Gen 22:12). So even if Abraham may have understood the command to present his son as a burnt offering, God had no such intention. Instead, his purpose was simply to test Abraham's faith. Since the deed was not carried out, there is nothing unworthy of divine goodness in having instituted the trial of his faith.

The testing may have had a greater benefit to Abraham than we often suppose. Some, such as the ancient Bishop Warburton, supposed that Abraham wanted to know how it was that God would bless all the families of the earth through his seed as promised in Genesis 12:3. On this supposition, it is conjectured that our Lord designed a way to teach him through an experience what he had already communicated to him in words. He was given a prefiguration, or a type, of the sacrifice that the last in the line of the seed, even Christ, would accomplish.

John 8:56 substantiates this claim when Jesus said, "Your father Abraham rejoiced at the thought of seeing my day; he saw
it and was glad." The reply of the Jewish audience, "You are not
yet fifty years old, . . . and you have seen Abraham!" (8:57),
indicates that they understood the verb *to see* in a most literal
way. Our Lord does not correct them in the notion they had
formed of seeing. But it must be noticed that it was not he
himself that Christ asserted that Abraham rejoiced to see, but his
day, by which he meant the circumstance of his life which was
of the greatest importance.

That the term *day* will permit this interpretation is clear from
the parallel words *hour* and *time*. Throughout the Gospels we
read, "his time has not yet come" (Jn 7:30); "he . . . prayed that
if possible the hour might pass from him" (Mk 14:35); or "the
hour has come for the Son of Man to be glorified" (Jn 12:23). In
all of these instances not a mere portion of time is being referred
to but some particular life circumstance unique to him and his
mission.

But if *day* functions in the same manner as *hour*, and the peculiar circumstance referred to is the one in which Jesus became
the Savior of the world, where is it recorded in the Old Testament that Abraham saw anything pertaining to the death of
Christ?

Nothing in the Old Testament says in so many words that
Abraham saw the death of Messiah as the Savior of the world.
It is possible, however, that what our Lord is referring to is the
transaction in Genesis 22 when Abraham was asked to sacrifice
his only son on Mount Moriah. In fact, this is the only event to
which it could possibly refer.

In this event of offering his son, Abraham would have had a
lively figure of the future offering of the Son of God as a sacrifice
for the sins of the world. Several factors point to this conclusion:
(1) the place where the binding of Isaac took place was "the

region of Moriah" (a land which included the site of Jerusalem and a well-known mountain by the same name); (2) the distance to which Abraham is asked to go is most unusual if the purpose was simply to test his faith (a test which could have been accomplished many miles closer to home than the Jerusalem area where he was sent by God); and (3) the fact that Isaac was the promised seed who bore in his person and in his life the promise of all that God was going to do in the future.

There are two kinds of child or human sacrifice known in the Old Testament. There were, first of all, those sacrifices of children or older individuals offered either as a building sacrifice at the laying of the cornerstone of a city and its gates (1 Kings 16:34) or in a particular time of crisis, such as when a city was under siege or in imminent prospect of being captured (2 Kings 3:27; Mic 6:7). Probably this category should also include sacrifices of individuals as a gift to the pagan gods for granting victory (Judg 11) and the taking of prisoners of war for sacrifice.

But this is separate from the sacrifice required in the Old Testament of all the firstborn (Ex 13:12-13; 34:19-20; Num 3:44-51). Of course it must be hastily added that nowhere in Scripture did God require the sacrifice of persons as he did of animals and the produce of the field; instead he took one Levite for service at the temple for the eldest son in each household as a substitute for the life which was owed to God.

As stated earlier, God has the right to require human sacrifice. All biblical sacrifice rests on the idea that the gift of life to God, either in consecration or in expiation, is necessary to restore the broken fellowship with God caused by sin. What passes from man to God is not regarded as property belonging to us but only what is symbolically regarded as property and thus is the gift of life of the offerer.

However, the offerer is in no shape, because of sin, to make such a gift. Thus the principle of vicariousness is brought into play: one life takes the place of another. Accordingly, Abraham is asked by God to offer life, the life that is dearest to him, his only son's. But in the provision of God, a ram caught in the thicket is interposed by the angel of the Lord, thus pointing out that the substitution of one life for another is indeed acceptable to God and that is what relieves us from sacrificing average sinful life. God, however, reserves the right to give his own Son, the perfect human life. But this in no way gives comfort to the devotees of nature-worship systems whose alleged deities were subject to life and death and who therefore wrongly required their worshipers to immolate themselves or their children to achieve fellowship with these nonbeings.

CHAPTER 12

I Will Bless You Because Abraham Obeyed My Laws

I will be with you and will bless you. For to you and your descendants I will give all these lands. . . . I will make your descendants as numerous as the stars in the sky and will give them all these lands, and through your offspring all nations on the earth will be blessed, because Abraham obeyed me and kept my requirements, my commands, my decrees and my laws.

GENESIS 26:3-5

Did God grant his gracious gifts to Abraham on the basis of works? Are we to surmise that Old Testament men and women got salvation the old-fashioned Smith-Barney way: "They earned it"?

It is the word *because* in Genesis 26:3-5 that causes us to raise our eyebrows and see this as a hard saying. There does appear to be a tension here between the free and unconditional offer of the promise to Abraham and the promise conditioned on Abraham's keeping all God's commands, decrees and laws. Surely law and grace are on a theological collision course.

There are five key passages that are cited as demonstrating that the patriarch Abraham performed the requirements of God and in return God offered to him the everlasting covenant as a gift for his obedience: Genesis 12:1; 17:1, 9-14; 22:16; 26:3-5. Some have added additional commands to this list, but generally these are not as directly related to the promise-plan as the five already cited.

The difficulty that this argument for conditionality and earning the promise is the stress the text makes on God actively conferring this covenant on Abraham. In one of the most dramatic scenes in the patriarch's life, Genesis 15:12-21 depicts Abraham as being only a passive party to the covenant which is being formalized, while the Lord, appearing as a "smoking firepot with a blazing torch," passes between the pieces of the animals in the act of making a covenant with Abraham. It is well worth noting that only God passed between the pieces and therefore obligated himself. Had this been a bilateral covenant in which the covenant depended equally on both parties fulfilling their sides of the bargain, then both God and Abraham would have had to move between the pieces of the animals divided in half and say in effect, "May it happen to me what has happened to these animals if I do not uphold my side of the covenant."

So how shall we explain the seeming disparity which now seems to intrude, requiring obedience from Abraham if the covenant is to be maintained?

The answer will be this: promise and blessing still precede the command to obey and to keep the commands of God. Obedience is no more a condition for Abraham than it is for the church living under the command, "If you obey my commands, you will remain in my love" (Jn 15:10) or "If you love me, you will obey what I command" (Jn 14:15).

The promise does not oppose God's law, either in Abraham's gift of the promise or in our gift of eternal life. The promise-giver who initiated the covenant with the patriarchs is the same one who gave the commandments, laws and statutes. Obedience, then, was not a condition for receiving the promise-blessing of God but was instead the evidence of real participation in that same promise. Because God was faithful, it was possible for these patriarchs to receive the promised blessings even if they themselves did not participate in them through their own belief. Even those who were not personal participants in the benefits of the covenant still had to pass on these benefits to those who followed in the line of the seed of the patriarchs. That belief was most easily demonstrated by the way in which individuals obeyed God—just as John puts it in his Gospel for the believing community of the New Testament.

Therefore, the alleged conditional elements in the Abrahamic (and Davidic) covenant never threatened the constituent elements of the promise, nor did they add any stipulations to them. The matter of duty or obedience, which indeed is intimately bound up with the promise, is a matter of outcome and sequel rather than a prior condition to being a participant in its benefits by faith.

The most remarkable text expressing the unconditional nature of the promise is Leviticus 26:44-45—"Yet in spite of this [the sins of disobedience], . . . I will not reject them or abhor them so as to destroy them completely, breaking my covenant with them. But for their sake I will remember the covenant with their ancestors. . . ." Surely, that sounds as if it is indeed an unconditional covenant!

CHAPTER 13

You Intended to Harm Me, But God Intended It for Good

*But Joseph said to [his brothers], "Don't be
afraid. Am I in the place of God? You
intended to harm me, but God intended it for
good to accomplish what is now being
done, the saving of many lives."*
GENESIS 50:19-20

How can God be God if individuals are truly free to make their own choices? It would appear that sooner or later these two free agents would collide head-on and one would need to give place to the other.

This passage has comforted many and helped them better understand how the principles of divine sovereignty, human freedom and individual responsibility relate to each other. It affirms that divine sovereignty and human freedom operate in ways that are sometimes surprising.

God hates all sin with a perfect and an unremitting hatred. However, it is his prerogative to allow good to come out of the evil others devise. Indeed, no sin can be committed without his knowledge or against his holy will. In this sense, sinners are often just as much the ministers of his providential workings as are his saints.

When because of jealousy and deep hatred Joseph's half brothers sold Joseph into slavery, God by his own mysterious working sent him to Egypt, not only to save that pagan nation (proof of common grace available to all by virtue of the decrees of creation) but to save the very people who sold him into those horrible circumstances. By so doing, Joseph attained the position his brothers were attempting to undermine. And ultimately God was glorified.

Accordingly, Joseph was taught to acknowledge and revere God's providence in his circumstances. He taught his brothers to share these same truths. They and we are to view God's hand not only in his goodness and mercy to us, but in our afflictions and trials as well.

Sinners cannot undo their actions or prevent the natural consequences of sin from producing its usual miserable effects, but there are innumerable occasions to thank a gracious Lord for counteracting and mitigating the otherwise devastating effects of such evil. God can and does work all things for good to those who love him and who are called according to his purposes to be transformed into his Son's image (Rom 8:28-29).

Such a confession does not mean that the nature of sin is altered and that believers never experience pain caused by sin. Poison does not cease to be poison just because it can sometimes be used medicinally.

However, this text claims that God need not worry that his purposes will be countermandated by society's sinful actions. Nor will God have to limit the freedoms which all individuals have, both believers and unbelievers, in order to preserve his sovereignty. He can cope with it and he does succeed. The result is that

God remains God and individuals remain responsible, blameworthy and culpable for all their acts.

There is both a directive will of God as well as a permissive will
in the divine purpose. Men and women may be culpable and
blameworthy for an act such as crucifying the Lord of glory, but
as a permitted act it can still come under the total plan of God.
As Acts 2:23 states, "This man [Jesus] was handed over to you
by God's set purpose and foreknowledge; and you, with the help
of wicked men, put him to death by nailing him to the cross." If
that is true for Christ's crucifixion, then it is no less true in the
case of Joseph and all similarly besieged men and women today.

· C H A P T E R 1 4 ·

A Three-Day Journey to Offer Sacrifices to the Lord

*Then you and the elders are to go to the king of
Egypt and say to him, "The LORD, the God
of the Hebrews, has met with us. Let us take a
three-day journey into the desert to offer
sacrifices to the LORD our God."*
EXODUS 3:18

Is this an example of a half-truth or a ruse which was intended to deceive
Pharaoh? In other words, is Israel's request of a three-day wilderness trip to worship God only an excuse to leave Egypt in order to make a break for Palestine before Pharaoh's troops could easily follow?

Since this pagan king would never submit his will to God's, would Moses and the Hebrew elders have been justified in tricking him as long as they got the children of Israel out of town? After all, does not the end justify the means? Or if that appears to be too casuistic for believers, should not Moses and the elders have chosen the lesser evil or perhaps even the greater good?

Each of these options has been offered in ethical theory. But each raises a different set of problems for the Christian. Even the appeal to Psalm 18:26 by Rabbi Rashi misses the point, "With the crooked [some interpreted to mean *with Pharaoh]* you [God] are crafty." But we object that divine judgment never came until Pharaoh had rejected all divine appeals to acquiesce to God's plan. Instead, the best solution was proposed long ago by the fourth-century A.D. church father Augustine and the fifteenth-century Spanish exegete Abarbanel. In their view, God deliberately graded his requests of Pharaoh by first placing before him a fairly simple plea that the people of Israel be allowed a three-day journey into the wilderness after which they would return. True, this first plea would lead to requests increasingly more difficult for Pharaoh to grant; however, they would each prepare Pharaoh to do what he might otherwise be unprepared to do.

Had Pharaoh complied with this request, the Israelites could not have exceeded the bounds of this permission. After returning to Egypt they would have needed to present a series of such pleas leading to the final request for full release. Here we can see God's tender love and concern for Pharaoh. This king is more than just a pawn in the plan of God. And Israel was responsible to honor the "powers that be."

Remarkably, God warns Moses that the king of Egypt will deny the request. Thus God knows both what actually takes place and what could have taken place. This warning confirms Amos 3:7: "Surely the Lord God does nothing without revealing his plan to his servants the prophets" (RSV). Not even God's "mighty hand" of miracles, evidenced in the plagues, will budge Pharaoh's obduracy and recalcitrance.

One further question might be posed here: Did not Moses, under the instigation of Yahweh, deliberately mislead Pharaoh when he concealed his real intention? If Moses ultimately intended to ask Pharaoh to release the Israelites, did not this concealment constitute a half-truth? In other words, is not the essence of falsehood the intention to deceive? If Pharaoh received the impression that Moses wanted only to journey far enough away to sacrifice without offending the Egyptians (they would sacrifice animals sacred in Egypt), are not Moses and God telling lies?

No! There is a vast difference between telling a lie and concealing information that others have forfeited a right to know because of their hostile attitude toward God or his moral standards. King Saul, for example, forfeited his right to know all the reasons for the prophet Samuel's visit, which was actually to anoint David the next king (1 Sam 16:1-2).

Likewise, in certain situations, such as sports or warfare, part of the objective is concealing as much of one's activities as possible. It would seem silly for a Christian to refuse to fake a play, saying, "No you don't; I'm a Christian and I have a testimony to maintain. Either give me the football or I won't run!"

We may now sharpen our definition of lying to mean the intentional deception of an individual who has the right to know the truth from us, and under circumstances in which he or she has a claim to such knowledge. The point is that lying is more than an intentional deception. Such deception may be a moral evil, but one cannot tell this until it is determined if such individuals have a claim to all or even part of the truth. Therefore, all men and women always have an obligation to speak only the truth, but they do not have an obligation always to speak up or tell everything they know just because they are asked—especially when some have forfeited their right to know the truth by flouting the truth they already possess.

· C H A P T E R 1 5 ·

The Lord Hardened Pharaoh's Heart

But the LORD hardened Pharaoh's heart and
he would not listen to Moses and Aaron,
just as the LORD had said to Moses.
EXODUS 9:12

T*he theme of "hardening" occurs twenty times between Exodus 4 and*
14. But the most troublesome aspect of these verses is that God
himself is said to have hardened Pharaoh's heart in ten out of the
twenty occurrences. This fact troubles many readers of the
Scriptures, for it appears God authors evil and then holds someone else responsible as if the person had initiated the evil. Did
God make it impossible for Pharaoh to respond and then find
Pharaoh guilty for such grotesque behavior?

God twice predicts he will harden Pharaoh's heart. These two
prophetic notices were given to Moses before the whole contest
began (Ex 4:21; 7:3). However, if these two occurrences appear

to cast the die against Pharaoh, it must be remembered that all God's prophecies to his prophets have a suppressed "unless you repent" attached to them. Few prophecies are unconditional. These include God's covenant with the seasons in Genesis 8:22; his covenant with Abraham, Isaac, Jacob and David; his New Covenant; and his covenant with the New Heavens and the New Earth in Isaiah 65—66.

In general, only his promises connected with nature and our salvation have no dependence on us; all others are much like Jonah's message to Nineveh. Even though Jonah never even hinted at the fact that their imminent destruction (only forty days away) could be avoided by repentance, the king assumed such was the case and Jonah's worst fears were realized: the nation repented and the barbarous Assyrians did not get what was coming to them!

In Pharaoh's case, Pharaoh initiated the whole process by hardening his own heart ten times during the first five plagues (Ex 7:13, 14, 22; 8:15, 19, 32; 9:7, 34, 35; and in 13:15). It was always and only Pharaoh who hardened his heart during these plagues! Rather than letting the work of God soften his heart during these plagues and concluding that Yahweh is the only true God, Pharaoh made this evidence the basis for hardening his heart. Meanwhile, the plagues must have had some impact on the general population of Egypt, for when the Israelites left Egypt, they were accompanied by "many other people" (Ex 12:38). Even Pharaoh's own magicians confessed, "This is the finger [the work] of God" (Ex 8:19), and they bowed out of the competition with the living God.

It appears that Pharaoh reached the limits of his circumscribed freedom during the fifth plague, for after that time, during the last five plagues, God consistently initiated the hardening instead of Pharaoh (Ex 9:12; 10:1, 20, 27; 11:10; 14:4, 8, 17).

God is not the author of evil. There is no suggestion that he

violated the freedom of Pharaoh's will or that God manipulated
Pharaoh in order to heap further vengeance on the Egyptian
people. God is not opposed to the cooperation of pagan monarchs. Pharaoh could have cooperated with God just as Cyrus did
in the Babylonian exile; God was still glorified when that king
decided on his own to let Israel return from Babylon. If Pharaoh
had acted as King Cyrus would later do, the results of the exodus
would still have been the same. It is Pharaoh, not God, who is
to be blamed for the hardening of his own heart.

• C H A P T E R 1 6 •

The Israelites
Plundered
the Egyptians

*The Israelites did as Moses instructed and asked
the Egyptians for articles of silver and
gold for clothing. The LORD had made the
Egyptians favorably disposed toward the
people, and they gave them what
they asked for; so they plundered the Egyptians.*
EXODUS 12:35-36

Three separate passages in Exodus record the narrative generally referred to as the spoiling of the Egyptians (Ex 3:21-22; 11:2-3; 12:35-36). The problems associated with the passages are partly a modern translation problem, which existed in most translations until just recently, and partly the question of whether Israel deceived the Egyptians by borrowing clothing and jewelry they would never return. How could God have commanded them to borrow items when he knew the Israelites would never return with them?

Let us first address the verb sometimes translated *to borrow*. This verb can as easily be rendered "to ask for something with no thought of return" (Judg 8:24; 1 Sam 1:28). Accordingly, the third-century B.C. Greek translation of the Septuagint and the Latin Vulgate translated it: "to ask." This same Hebrew word is occasionally translated "to borrow," as in Exodus 22:14 or 2 Kings 4:3 and 6:5. In these instances, context determines its rendering.

In this case, the context also contains the verb *to plunder* which appears in Exodus 3:22 and 12:36. Here the meaning is clear, as it is in 2 Chronicles 20:25. It is a military metaphor which could, in some contexts, imply taking things by force, but never by fraud, deceit or any kind of a ruse or cunning device. It is not, however, the usual term for plundering the enemy.

The background for this thrice-recorded incident is the ancient promise God had given to Abraham in Genesis 15:14 that the Hebrews would leave Egypt "with great possessions." God repeated this promise to Moses: Israel would "not go empty-handed" (Ex 3:20-21) away from Egypt.

God himself favorably disposed the hearts of the Egyptians toward Israel (Ps 106:46 says, "he caused them to be pitied"). Also Moses was "highly regarded" (Ex 11:3) by the Egyptians. However, such esteem was not solely attributable to Moses' personal qualifications, though he had garnered quite a reputation with the magicians (Ex 8:18-19), the court officials (Ex 9:20; 10:7) and Pharaoh himself (Ex 9:27; 10:16). The general populace of Egypt recognized that God was with this man and his people. Therefore, a great outpouring of generosity ensued and that is what these three texts record. All the Israelites had to do was ask. The people were so ready to acknowledge that Israel indeed had been mistreated and that God had been remarkably present with the Jewish leadership that they gave openhandedly.

Notice that the women did not ask for such objects as weapons, armor, cattle, food supplies or goods for the home, table or job occupations. To avoid all suggestions in this direction, the author of Psalm 105:37 may have dropped the word *articles* before the words *silver and gold* so as not to imply that the Israelites asked for a third group of things besides the jewels and clothing.

This type of spoiling is not the usual term used of plundering someone who has fallen in battle. When one adds that the Egyptians willingly surrendered their jewels and articles of silver and gold, the apparent moral problem is resolved. One can guess that the Egyptians viewed their gifts as partial compensation for the grief and toil the Hebrews endured during their centuries of slavery in that land.

No legitimate moral questions remain once the situation is understood as a straightforward request which the Egyptians answered only too gladly, for by now almost everyone sympathized with their cause.

· CHAPTER 17 ·

Eye for Eye, Tooth for Tooth

But if there is serious injury, you are to take
life for life, eye for eye, tooth for tooth,
hand for hand, foot for foot, burn for burn,
wound for wound, bruise for bruise.
EXODUS 21:23-25

Lex talionis, *"law of the tooth," or the so-called law of retaliation,* is found here in Exodus 21:23-25 in its fullest form. It is preserved in a shorter form in Leviticus 24:19-20 and Deuteronomy 19:21. The issue this law raises is: Were the Israelites allowed to practice private vendettas and to retaliate every time they were personally wronged?

This legislation was never intended to allow individuals to avenge their own injuries. It is included in the section of Exodus addressed to the "judges" (Ex 21:1—22:17). These laws functioned, then, as precedents for the civil and criminal magistrates in settling disputes and administering justice, but they were not to be applied in a wooden or literalistic way.

Simply stated, the *talion* principle was "life for life." But in actuality this rule functioned as a stereotyped expression for the judges who had to assign compensations and amounts of restitution in damage cases. If the law were pressed too literally, it was misunderstood and became an unmanageable concept conjuring up images of the most gross and barbarous infliction of recriminating justice on a society gone mad!

But if one jumps to the conclusion that the Bible authorized physical mutilation, the biblical rejection and proscription against any such personal vendetta is clearly set forth in Exodus 21:26-27, the very next verses of our passage.

The expression *eye for eye and tooth for tooth* simply meant that the compensations paid were to match the damages inflicted—no more and no less. The modern version would be, "bumper for bumper, fender for fender"—don't try to get two years' free tuition added on the insurance claim by some phony story about whiplash or imagined ailments.

In modern law, such terms as *damages* or *compensation* usually replace the term *restitution*. In modern law an offense is seen as against the state or one's neighbor; in biblical law the offense was seen as against God as well.

Even in those cases where life was literally required as the punishment for the offense, a substitution was available, as Numbers 35:31 implies. This text specifies that no ransom is available for murder, implying that a commensurate compensation might be possible in cases other than first degree murder. The Hebrew verb for *to give* appears in Exodus 21:23; in the surrounding verses, this verb refers to monetary compensation (see Exodus 21:19, 22, 30, 32). The ordinary verb that is used for restoring in kind, or paying the exact equivalent, is the verb *to make whole* or repay.

The earlier stages of biblical law did not distinguish as sharply as present legislators do between criminal law (determining punishment) and civil law (determining commensurate compensation). If this is so, then Exodus 21:23-25 is not a *lex talionis*, a law of retaliation, but a formula for compensation or composition. Moreover, the principle of equivalence also applies. It appears at this point because it applies not only to the laws preceding it (theft), but also to the laws following it (assault); indeed, it applies even to third parties who were drawn involuntarily into a clash.

A literal interpretation of *hand for hand* may not be a fair and equivalent compensation if one man was a singer and the other a pianist. The formula "hand for hand" must be understood conceptually to mean "the means of livelihood for the means of livelihood."

Interpreters must be careful not to fall into the ditch on either side of this issue: (1) the danger of transferring to the private sector what these verses assigned solely and properly to the judges; or (2) an overliteralizing tendency which fails to see that this principle comes under the heading of restitution and not retaliation, that the compensation was to fit the damages—no more and no less. In fact, while some have thought that this text condoned excessive retribution, it actually curbed all retribution and any personal retaliation among Israel's citizens.

• C H A P T E R   1 8 •

If You Lend, Charge No Interest

*If you lend money to one of my people
among you who is needy, do not
be like a moneylender; charge
him no interest.*

EXODUS 22:25

Discussion about money divides friends, and when it comes to talking
about interest on money from a biblical point of view, it divides
interpreters! To be sure, the "one who lends his [or her] money
without usury [interest]," according to Psalm 15:5, "does not
accept a bribe against the innocent." But what is not immediately
noticed is that the borrower is usually described as one who is
in need and who is unable to support himself or herself. That
point is made in two of the three main teaching passages on this
topic, namely Exodus 22:25 and Leviticus 25:35-37. (The third
passage is Deut 23:19-20.)

The reason for such a stern prohibition against charging inter-

est was that all too many in Israel used this method to avoid
helping the poor and their own fellow citizens. Deuteronomy
23:20 did say, "You may charge a foreigner interest." Apparently,
this was the same as charging interest for a business loan or an
investment, which also was allowed in Matthew 25:27. The foreigner fell under the category of the "resident alien" who had
taken up permanent residence among the Israelites. But where
the law protected a "resident alien" with the same privileges
granted a native Israelite, we may expect the same prohibitions
against loaning at interest to the poor (see Lev 25:35).

Of course, all morality condemned excessive rates of interest.
Warned Proverbs 28:8, "He who increases his wealth by exorbitant interest amasses it for another, who will be kind to the
poor." The prophet Ezekiel also described the "righteous person"
as one who "does not lend at usury or take excessive interest"
(Ezek 18:8, see also 13, 17; 22:12).

What has changed the sentiment in modern times on legitimate forms of interest-taking is an altered perception of the
nature and use of money. In the first place, loans today are most-
ly needed for quite different purposes. In that day it was a matter
of extreme and dire need which would force a person into the
position of needing to borrow. In these cases, what was owed to
one another was compassion. They were to help one another, not
use their neighbor's calamity as the opportunity to realize quick
and illegitimate profits.

In modern times, loans are required principally as a means of
increasing the capital with which one works. Unless one has the
increased capital, that particular industry may not be capable of
bringing in the increased revenue. But in ancient times, such
concerns were not as large as they have become in the modern
era. Loans then were almost exclusively for the purpose of re-
lieving destitution and extreme poverty.

While Hebrew uses two different terms for *interest*, it is doubtful one can distinguish between them, such as between a long-term and short-term loan, or an exorbitant rate of interest versus a fair rate of return for the use of one's money. Neither can it be said that one relates to the substance loaned and the other to the method by which the loan was computed.

It is a reasonable conclusion that interest was and is still approved for those ventures not attempting to circumvent one's obligation to the poor. This thesis is reinforced by Jesus' allusion to and apparent approval of taking interest for commercial ventures in Matthew 25:27 and Luke 19:23.

The appropriateness of loaning money to a church or a Christian nonprofit agency at interest is also greatly debated. Some counsel that ministries that invite "investments" with the offer to pay back the principal with interest may well end up paying the interest out of the tithes, thus robbing God.

If the reason for the prohibition on all church loans is that believers are not to be charged interest, then we must demur since that is not the biblical reason. Scripture is concerned about our dodging our responsibilities to the poor in our midst. The absolute prohibition of lending at interest to believers will not stand scriptural scrutiny. This is not to say that there are no other traps in this whole discussion. There are. The abuse of the tithe would be a most serious matter. However, because ministries seem to grow in proportion to their facilities, a group may choose to build ahead in order to expand their ministry and at the same time their base of supporters. Such an expansion is not only warranted but is a legitimate and responsible exercise of good Christian stewardship.

The Bible is anxious mainly about a profiteer's loan which should have been a charity loan at no interest. Once that demand has been met, other principles in Christian morality must be met as well, but the pressure will no longer be to decry all forms of interest-taking as such.

CHAPTER 19

Tablets of Stone Inscribed with the Finger of God

*When the LORD finished speaking to Moses
on Mount Sinai, he gave him the two tablets of
the Testimony, the tablets of stone inscribed
by the finger of God.*
EXODUS 31:18

Readers of the New Testament know that *"God is spirit, and his* worshipers must worship in spirit and in truth" (Jn 4:24). But this same incorporeal argument for God is in the Old Testament: "But the Egyptians are men and not God; their horses are flesh and not spirit" (Is 31:3). Clearly God and spirit are balancing concepts in the Hebrew poetic device called synonymous parallelism. How, then, can Moses describe God as having fingers to write on the tablets of stone?

Since God is not corporeal in the sense that he has bodily form (Is 31:3; Jn 4:24), all references to parts of the body such as fingers are what we call anthropomorphisms—something about the divine person more graphically told in human terms.

The *finger of God* is also a figure of speech known as *synecdoche*, wherein a portion of the divine person is used to denote some larger aspect of his person or characteristics. In this case God's power is being indicated by his finger.

Accordingly, the magicians bowed out after the third plague, stating, "This is the finger of God [or of a god]" (Ex 8:19). Clearly, by their use of the word *finger* they meant they had been outmaneuvered by a supernatural power that was at work, not by some kind of cheap trickery or quackery.

Some have argued, on the alleged bases of Egyptian parallels, such as chapter 153 in the Egyptian *Book of the Dead*, that *finger of God* refers literally to Aaron's staff. This theory, which also presupposes an artificial distinction between the singular and plural forms for *finger*, is arbitrarily supported. The statement of these Egyptian magicians, therefore, attributes to God the power they had just observed in the third plague.

God's power is again symbolized as the "work of [his] fingers" in creating the world, according to the psalmist (Ps 8:3). What is more, it was by the same "finger of God" that Jesus claimed to have cast demons out of individuals in Luke 11:20. We may be confident, then, that the term *finger of God* refers to his power.

The use of this expression in connection with the writing of the Ten Commandments on the two tablets of stone is most interesting, for while we do not believe in a mechanical view of dictation for the Bible, nevertheless this passage certainly indicates that here is one passage that is in some ways markedly different from the other portions of Scripture which are nonetheless just as inspired. It must mean that this passage came, in some way, through to the direct intervening power of God. Perhaps we are to envision something approximating the handwriting on the wall at Belshazzar's Babylonian feast in Daniel 5:5. Some have likened it to a bolt of lightning which engraved the stones by a supernatural power.

The truth is that no one knows the method for sure, but we do know it is as much a product of the direct power of God as Jesus' miracles or his creation of the world. This part of the law known as the "Two Tablets of the Testimony" were the result of the direct intervention of God, most graphically described as the "finger of God."

· C H A P T E R 2 0 ·

You Will See My Back; But My Face Must Not Be Seen

*And the LORD said, "I will cause all my goodness to pass
in front of you, and I will proclaim my name, the LORD,
in your presence. I will have mercy on whom I will have mercy,
and I will have compassion on whom I will have compassion. But,"
he said, "you cannot see my face, for no one may see
me and live." Then the LORD said, "There is a place
near me where you may stand on a rock. When my glory passes
by, I will put you in a cleft in the rock and cover you with
my hand until I have passed by. Then I will remove my hand
and you will see my back; but my face must not be seen."*
EXODUS 33:19-23

If no one can see God and still live, how may we interpret those texts which
seem to say the opposite, including this text referring to God's
"back"?

On one hand, some texts say God was seen. Genesis 32:30
remarks, "So Jacob called the place Peniel, saying, 'It is because
I saw God face to face.' " Exodus 24:9-10 likewise teaches that
"Moses and Aaron, Nadab and Abihu, and the seventy elders of
Israel . . . saw the God of Israel." Exodus 33:11 strikes another

intimate note: "The LORD would speak to Moses face to face, as
a man speaks with his friend." Judges 13:22 states that Manoah
said to his wife, "We are doomed to die! . . . We have seen God!"
Again, in Isaiah 6:1, "In the year that King Uzziah died, I saw
the Lord seated on a throne, high and exalted." Finally, Daniel
7:9 affirms, "As I looked, thrones were set in place, and the
Ancient of Days took his seat. His clothing was as white as
snow; the hair of his head was white like wool. His throne was
flaming with fire." All these texts appear to claim that at times
God can be seen and was seen.

However, there are other passages that appear to argue that
it is impossible to see God. Foremost among them is our text,
Exodus 33:20. Likewise, Deuteronomy 4:15 warns, "You saw no
form of any kind the day the LORD spoke to you at Horeb out
of the fire." Even more to the point was John 1:18, "No one has
ever seen God, but God the One and Only, who is at the Father's
side, has made him known." And again in John 5:37, "You have
never heard his voice nor seen his form." Indeed, God is described in 1 Timothy 1:17 as "the King eternal, immortal, invis-
ible," the one "whom no one has seen or can see" (1 Tim 6:16).

To resolve this dilemma, note first that some of these sightings
are visions, such as the cases of Isaiah and Daniel. In others, the
terms for *sight* stress the directness of access. For instance, in
Exodus 24:9-11, Moses, Aaron, Nadab, Abihu and the seventy
elders eat and drink in God's presence but they describe only his
feet and what he stood on. Probably, they were not permitted to
look on God's face. In another instance, Jacob's access to God is
described as being "face to face," similar to Moses' later friend-
ship with God. (The difference may arise from the way the term
face of God was used in various contexts. In one, it expressed
familiarity beyond previous visions or divine appearances; in others, it referred to knowledge of God which exceeds our abilities
and hopes.) Others, such as Manoah and his wife, experienced

a Christophany or a theophany, which means an appearance of Christ or God through a vision or a preincarnate appearance.

What Moses requests in Exodus 33:18, "Now show me your glory" was more than the Lord would grant for Moses' own good. Even so, God allowed his "goodness" to pass in front of Moses and proclaimed his "name" in Moses' presence.

Thus, instead of showing Moses his person or describing his appearance, the Lord gave Moses a description of who he is. The "name" of God included his nature, character (Ps 20:1; Lk 24:47; Jn 1:12), doctrine (Ps 22:22; Jn 17:6, 26) and standards for living righteously (Mic 4:5). Romans 9:15 quotes this verse from Exodus and applies it to God's sovereignty.

After God proclaims his name and sovereignty, he promises Moses a look at certain of his divine aspects. What these aspects were is still debated—needlessly, when one considers the range of meaning for the word *back* or the context in which it is used.

God placed Moses in a cleft in the rock, apparently a cavelike crevice, and he then caused his glory to pass by. The glory of God refers first and foremost to the sheer weight or the reality of his presence. The presence of God would come near Moses in spatial terms.

But Moses would not be able to endure the spectacular purity, luminosity and reality of staring at the raw glory of God himself. Instead, God would protect Moses from accidental (and apparently, fatal) sight of that glory. Therefore, in a striking anthropomorphism (a description of the reality of God in terms or analogies understandable to mortals), God would protect Moses from the full effects of looking directly at the glory of God by placing his hand over Moses' face until all God's glory had passed by.

That this is a figure of speech is clear from the double effect of God passing by and while simultaneously protecting Moses with the divine "hand." Only after his glory, or presence, had

passed by would God remove his gracious, protecting "hand."
Then Moses would view what God had permitted.

But what was left for Moses to see? The translators say God's
back. But since God is spirit (Is 31:3; Jn 4:24) and formless, what
would this refer to? The word *back* can as easily be rendered the
aftereffects of the glory that had passed by.

This would fit the context as well as the range of meanings for
the Hebrew word used. Moses did not see the glory of God
directly, but once it had gone past, God did allow him to view the
results, the afterglow, that his presence had produced.

CHAPTER 21

The Man Who Obeys My Laws Will Live by Them

*Keep my decrees and laws, for the man
who obeys them will live by them.
I am the LORD.*
LEVITICUS 18:5

T his saying's importance is assured by its appearance in such later
contexts as Ezekiel 20:11, Luke 10:28, Romans 10:5 and Galatians 3:12. But it is also a hard saying. The text appears to offer
an alternate method of gaining eternal life, even if only theoret-
ically. Is it true, in either the Old Testament or the New, that
a person could have eternal life by perfectly keeping the law of
God? In other words, can we read this saying: "Do this and you
will have [eternal] life"?

Unfortunately, all too many teachers of the Scriptures have
uncritically assumed that the words *live in them* meant that "eternal life was to be had by observing the laws of God." Accordingly,

if a person were to keep these commandments perfectly, the very keeping would be eternal life.

But this claim misses a major amount of contrary evidence, foremost that the benefits of God's promise-plan to the Old Testament believers was not conditioned on anything, much less on obedience. Such a position would reverse the unconditional word of blessing God gave to Abraham, Isaac, Jacob and David.

Some will reply, But what about the "if you obey me fully" statements of Exodus 19:5, Leviticus 26:3-13, and Deuteronomy 11:13-15 and 28:1? Do not these texts flatly declare that without obedience salvation is impossible?

The *if* is admittedly conditional, but conditional to what? It was conditional only to enjoyment of the full benefits of a relationship begun by faith and given freely by God. Israel must obey God's voice and heed his covenant and commandments, not "in order to" establish her new life in God, but "so that" (Deut 5:33) she might experience completely this new life begun in faith.

The very context of this verse speaks against a works salvation. First, Leviticus 18 begins and ends (vv. 2 and 30) with the theological assumption that the hearers have the Lord as their God. Thus, this instruction deals with sanctification rather than justification.

Second, "those things" which they were not to do were the customs and ordinances; in short, the pagan idolatries of the Egyptians and Canaanites. This is a whole world apart from the question of salvation.

Third, never in the Old or New Testaments has pleasing God constituted the external performance of acts; these acts carried with them the evidence of a prior attitude of the heart. For instance, circumcision of the flesh without the circumcision of the heart was wasted effort.

In fact, our Lord coupled the act and the heart when the people pledged, "All that the Lord says, we will do." Imperiously, some call such a pledge rash, judging the people foolish for falling for an offer they would never be able to live up to.

But our Lord did not see it that way. Rather, he said in so many words, "Oh that there were such an heart in them that they would always fear me and keep my commandments." Our Lord connects their "doing" with the "heart." He never reproved them by saying, "Oh, what deluded people! Given your previous track record, how on earth do you ever expect to enter my heaven by keeping any of my laws?" There is not a word about this. Therefore, this verse cannot be said to teach a hypothetical offer of salvation by works.

Some may argue that the words *live in them,* quoted in Romans 10:5 and Galatians 3:12, surely means in those contexts that salvation was "by means of" works (an instrumental use of the preposition). I shall respond that this expression should be translated live *in the sphere of them* (a locative use of the preposition).

Moses, therefore, was not describing the means of attaining salvation but only the horizon within which an earthly, godly life should be lived.

· C H A P T E R 2 2 ·

God Said Go
But Was Very Angry
Because He Went

*That night God came to Balaam and said, "Since
these men have come to summon you, go
with them, but do only what I tell you." Balaam
got up in the morning, saddled his donkey and
went with the princes of Moab. But God was
very angry when he went.*
NUMBERS 22:20-22

Was Balaam permitted to travel to the plains of Moab to curse
Israel, courtesy of Balak, King of Moab, or was he not? At first
blush, it appears to be a case where God gave his permission and
then turned back on what he had said.

This narrative has several surprising aspects. First of all, we
are shocked to learn a prophet of Yahweh was living in Upper
Mesopotamia, in the region where Abraham had stopped off at
Haran on his way from Ur of the Chaldees to the land of promise.

In fact, it is so amazing and unexpected that God would have
a non-Jewish prophet, it is widely supposed that Balaam was a
baru, a priest-diviner, who used the usual tricks of the trade, such

as dreams and omens, to forecast the future. But the Bible does not seem to support this, for Balaam used the name Yahweh, a name which implies a personal relationship ("He will be [there]").

Though Balak commissions him to curse the Israelites, it must be remembered that properly pronounced blessings and curses were also extremely effective in biblical teaching (Gen 48:14-20; Judg 17:1-2; Mt 21:18-22).

Was Balaam the embodiment of evil or was he basically a good man? Perhaps as is true of many others, he was a mixture of good and evil. He really knew the true, personal God of Israel, and like so many other believing Gentiles who receive only a passing reference in Scripture (such as Melchizedek, Jethro, Rahab), he too really believed to the saving of his soul. As a matter of fact, God not only used him to protect Israel from a curse, he was also the instrument of the great Messianic prophecies concerning the "Star out of Jacob," a guiding light for the Eastern wise men who later searched out the new king of the Jews.

How, then, shall we deal with the apparent contradiction in this passage? The solution lies in the text itself, not in suppositions or harmonizations.

Balaam had already received one royal delegation in Numbers 22:7-14. Balaam rightly replies that the Lord refused him permission to go with the princes of Moab to curse Israel. What Balaam had artfully neglected to mention was God's reason for refusing: "Because [Israel] is blessed" (Num 22:12). Mentioning this probably would have ended the Moabites' attempts to curse a people God blessed. Balaam apparently was playing both sides of the street on this one; he deliberately left the door open, perhaps hoping that he could somehow benefit from such a highly visible ministry.

As if anticipated, a second delegation returned to Balaam with an offer that amounted to a blank check. Now some have attempted to relieve the tension observed here by distinguishing between God and Yahweh. Balaam's pretensions of having Yahweh as his God (as in vv. 18 and 19) are exposed as phony, for it is not Yahweh who comes to him, but Elohim (v. 20). This solution is artificial, for verse 22 reports that it was Elohim who got angry. Champions of this theory note that the Samaritan Pentateuch and several important manuscripts of the Septuagint read *Yahweh* instead of *Elohim* in verse 22.

This may be true, but it still fails to see that the text itself does not make such a sharp distinction between God and Yahweh. Instead, the text stresses that the permission of Balaam was conditional. The King James Version phrases it, "If the men come to call thee, rise up, and go with them; yet the word which I shall say unto thee, that shalt thou do" (v. 20). Balaam, however, was all too anxious to go and did not wait for the men to call him; rather, he saddled his donkey and sought them out. The King James rendering of verse 20 is to be preferred to both the NIV's "Since the men have come . . ." and the RSV's "If the men have come . . ." because the very next verse, verse 21, makes it clear that Balaam initiated the action and did not wait for the test that God proposed to take effect. Verse 21 says, "Balaam got up in the morning, saddled his donkey and went with the princes of Moab." He "loved the wages of wickedness" (2 Pet 2:15).

Most commentators acknowledge that the proper force of the Hebrew *im* is "if"; however, they incorrectly reason that the men from Moab had already called and invited Balaam to go, thus there was no reason to suppose that any additional call was anticipated. Consequently, many treat the word *if* as a concessive particle with the meaning "since." What these scholars fail to realize is that Balaam had asked these men to spend the night while he made further investigations from the Lord.

This brief respite gave Balaam one more opportunity to sense God's will through his providential working—in this case, the disgust of the Moabite delegation, which would have packed up and left in the morning had not Balaam been so desirous of taking the job. Instead Balaam took the very initiative God had left in the hands of the Moabites ("*If* the men come") and thus evidenced his own disobedient inclinations.

Despite Balaam's strong declaration in verse 18 that, "Even if Balak gave me his palace filled with silver and gold, I could not do anything great or small to go beyond the command of the Lord my God," his mentioning both money and going beyond the will of God raises the question that this is exactly what he not only did, but planned to do if possible.

This passage, like many others, teaches us to differentiate between the directive and permissive will of God. God's directive will was clearly seen in the word, "Do not go with them . . . because they are blessed." This is so clear that it will admit no exceptions. But when Balaam continued to press God, God tested his willingness to obey (if it needed to be demonstrated that he had trouble knowing God's will). The test was a condition which depended on the discouraged princes returning one last time before leaving for home. However, Balaam could not wait, perhaps fearing they would not return. Only then was the anger of God excited.

The love of God did not cease at this point but was demonstrated in three more warnings from God that he was headed into trouble. Even though this was enough to straighten out Balaam for the immediate mission, it did not insulate him from future difficulties that God must have wished to spare Balaam.

The end of Balaam's ministry was tragic, for after he had served God by repeatedly blessing Israel, he became the instrument of both Israel's downfall and his own (Num 31:7-8, 15-16). But for this he had only himself to blame and not God, for he had been sternly warned. Sometimes God gives us the desires of our hearts, after we have begged and begged for a reversal of his will, but the result often is leanness for our spiritual lives.

Stone a Stubborn and Rebellious Son

*If a man has a stubborn and rebellious son who does not
obey his father and mother and will not listen to them
when they discipline him, his father and mother shall take hold
of him and bring him to the elders at the gate of his town.
They shall say to the elders, "This son of ours is stubborn and
rebellious. He will not obey us. He is a profligate
and a drunkard." Then all the men of his town shall stone
him to death. You must purge the evil from among you. All
Israel will hear of it and be afraid.*
DEUTERONOMY 21:18-21

At first glance, this law seems pitiless in its demands, both of a society
with incorrigibly delinquent children and of the emotionally torn
parents of such ruffians. But a second glance would question if
our pity is well placed. Shall we pity the criminal or the community? Does Scripture side with the offender or the offended? The
issue is not abstract nor antiquated. It haunts modern society as
well as the Christian community.

The case represented here particularizes the fifth of the Ten

Commandments. The sanctity of the family is at the heart of this command to honor one's parents. Accordingly, God's plan for the family in its origin, function and perpetuity was not to be measured by humanistic or societal conventions but by the counsel of God.

Children were to honor their parents as God's earthly representatives. To rebel against these representatives was equal to rebelling against God. In practice, obedience to parents (a command strictly qualified by "in the Lord") could then be transferred as obedience to God, for the parents taught the children the law of God. Parents were to impress the commandments of God on their children's hearts, while sitting together at home, walking along the road or getting up (Deut 6:6-7).

What happened when a serious case of juvenile delinquency appeared in the community? Should the family strike out in wrath to rid themselves of this embarrassment?

Deuteronomy 21:19-21 limits the power of the family. Parents were restricted to chastening and disciplining their children. They were never given power to kill or to abort life. Only under Roman law, as R. J. Rushdoony points out, was the parent the source and lord of life. In Scripture, God is the source and Lord over life.

Thus, when anyone in the extended family rebelled and refused to obey his or her parents (son does not restrict this law to sons, for it also included daughters and, by extension, all relatives), the rest of the family was to align themselves with God's law and not with the recalcitrant family member.

In fact, the family order was so sacred to the fabric of society and the plan of God that the accusing family members were not considered the complaining witnesses as in other cases. Ordinarily witnesses were required to participate in the execution by throwing the first stones (Deut 17:7). In this case, however, "all the men of his town" were required to participate, for the complaint was a complaint by the community against one of its members.

What disrupted one family in the community attacked the whole community. Moreover, if the parents had refused to bring the guilty and incorrigible individual to the elders, they would have been guilty of condoning and, in a sense, participating in the defiant son's crimes.

Did the town actually kill one of its own members just for being rebellious? Such behavior came under the curse of God himself, so serious was the charge of parental abuse by children or their defiant refusal to listen to them (Deut 27:16).

However, for each crime demanding capital punishment (except premeditated murder) there was a substitution or ransom that could be offered (Num 35:31). Thus, while the penalty marked the seriousness of the crime, the offer of a ransom would mitigate some of the severity in the actual sentencing. Scripture suggests no proper ransom or substitute in this case, but it likely was similar to contemporary sentencings which require community service for a specified time.

Could pity play any part in the sentencing of these crimes? Not if that pity were directed toward the violator rather than the violated or the word of God. Pity could distract people from serving God and honoring his word. There was to be no pity, for example, for the idolatrous worshipers of Canaan (Deut 7:16), the subverter of the faith (Deut 13:6- 9) or the coldblooded murderer (Deut 19:11-13). Instead, our affection ought to be toward the living God and what he has spoken. Any love, loyalty or pity which pre-empts that love is itself a lawless and faithless love.

· C H A P T E R 2 4 ·

I Do Not Know
Which Way
They Went

*But [Rahab] had taken the two men [spies from the Hebrews]
and hidden them. She said, "Yes, the men came to me,
but I did not know where they had come from. At dusk, when
it was time to close the city gate, the men left. I don't
know which way they went. Go after them quickly. You may catch
up with them." (But she had taken them up to the roof and hidden
them under the stalks of flax she had laid out on the roof.)*
JOSHUA 2:4-6

Does God approve of dubious actions to accomplish his will in certain
perilous situations? Can strong faith go hand in hand with the
employment of methods which are alien to the integrity of God's
character and word? Are Rahab's treason and lying in any way
justifiable, perhaps as a "white lie"?

The Bible is unhesitating in its praise of Rahab. Hebrews 11:31
praises her faith in God while James 2:25 praises her for lodging
and then sending off the spies in a different direction from those
seeking them. But approval of Rahab in these areas does not
mean that she enjoyed God's approval in every area of her life.
The areas of Rahab's faith must be strictly observed.

She won recognition by biblical writers because she trusted in the God of Israel more than she trusted her own king of Jericho. She had heard what God had done for Israel at the Red Sea and in defeating the two kings of the trans-Jordan (Josh 2:8-12). And she demonstrated her faith by receiving the spies and sending them out another way. Even Joshua 6:25 notes her actions and contrasts her response to that of Achan.

No guilt should be assigned, therefore, to her treason in abandoning her people, who like herself had great reason for trusting the God of the Hebrews. When it comes to choosing between serving God or a local king, the answer must always be to serve the higher power, God (Acts 4:19).

Her lie, on the other hand, cannot be so easily dismissed. She said, "I don't know which way they went." That was palpably false. Romans 3:8 warns us not to say, "Let us do evil that good may result." Neither should we argue, especially from a descriptive or a narrative passage, that a text validates deceit under certain conditions.

The so-called dutiful lie dismisses how precious the truth is in God's sight. Even lies told for very good purposes are not free from divine disapproval. Moreover, even if in the de facto providence of God, Rahab's untruth allowed the two spies to escape harm, this does not therefore justify such a method. God is not reduced to unholy acts to fulfill his will. At most, God allowed his purposes to be fulfilled in this most unusual manner, because his grace can operate in spite of the sinful maneuverings of men and women. Untruth cannot be vindicated simply because it is closely tied to the total result.

To argue for lying in this manner would not only be poor exegesis and theology but worse theodicy. Any other conclusion would eventually validate David's adultery because the next heir in the Messianic line, Solomon, resulted from David's union with Bathsheba. We are specifically told that David's sin was abhorrent to God. It happens we are not told the same about Rahab's sin. This is no reason to vote differently in the two cases; each violates a clear commandment of God.

We cannot say that protecting innocent lives is a greater good than the demand always to tell the truth. Scripture nowhere advocates or allows for such hierarchy. To do so would pit part of God's nature against other parts of his nature. To say that lying is a lesser evil than being involuntarily implicated in murder is again an artificial and subjective construct. We need to follow all of God's Word and that Word involves respect for both life and truth, as difficult as that is in a world that often pits one moral absolute against another.

Truth-telling is not only a covenantal responsibility (that is, a responsibility to those who are part of the family of God); it is a universal responsibility for all times, all peoples, in all places. We must not form our own subjective hierarchies or personal priorities in assigning what we believe is the greater good or lesser evil.

On the other hand, we may not surrender innocent lives just because an army or police force (such as Hitler's Third Reich) demands it. Rahab should have hidden the spies well and then refused to answer the question whether she was hiding them. She could, for instance, have volunteered, "Come in and have a look around," while simultaneously praying that God would make the searchers especially obtuse.

It is possible to maintain a position of nonconflicting absolutes. God will provide a way to avoid the conflicts (1 Cor 10:13).

· C H A P T E R   2 5 ·

It Was
the Angel
of the Lord

> *When Gideon realized that it was the angel of the*
> *LORD, he exclaimed, "Ah, Sovereign*
> *LORD! I have seen the angel of the LORD*
> *face to face!" But the LORD said to him, "Peace!*
> *do not be afraid. You are not going to die."*
> JUDGES 6:22-23

If *Gideon had only seen an angel, why did he fear that he might die?*
Many interpreters believe that an angel takes God's place and
acts as his representative, however others do not feel this explanation fits all the data. Who, then, is this angel of the Lord?

The angel of the Lord first appears in Genesis 16:7 and then
intermittently throughout the early Old Testament books. In
other passages, an individual manifesting himself in human form
is frequently called "the LORD" (Gen 12:7; 17:1; 18:1). Many believe, along with me, that the angel of the Lord is our Lord Jesus
Christ appearing in the Old Testament in human form.

If this angel actually were God, why is he called an angel? Since the root meaning of *angel* is "messenger, or one who is sent," we must determine from context whether the word refers to the *office* of the sent one or to the *nature* of created angels as finite beings.

Initially, some contexts of the term *angel of the* LORD appear to refer to nothing more than any other angel (as in Judg 6:11). But as the narrative progresses, that angel soon transcends the angelic category and is described in terms suited only to a member of the Trinity. Thus in the Judges 6 episode, we are startled when verse 14 has the Lord speaking to Gideon when previously only the angel of the Lord had been talking.

Many Old Testament passages state this angel is God. Thus, after being told that Hagar had been speaking with the angel of the Lord (four times in Gen 16:7, 9-11), verse 13 informs us that Hagar "gave this name to the LORD who spoke to her: 'You are the God who sees me.' " Jacob's testimony in Genesis 48:15-16 is even more striking. He identifies the God in whose presence his fathers Abraham and Isaac had lived as "the God who has been my shepherd all my life to this day, the Angel who has delivered me from all harm."

This angel spoke to Jacob earlier in a dream and identified himself by saying, "I am the God of Bethel, where you anointed a pillar and where you made a vow to me" (Gen 31:11, 13).

Likewise in Exodus 3:2-6 the phrase *the angel of the* LORD is used interchangeably with the term LORD. In fact, the angel claims, "I am the God of your father, the God of Abraham, the God of Isaac and the God of Jacob" (Ex 3:6).

In like manner, Judges 6:12 begins with the angel of the Lord, but as the narrative continues, verse 14 has the Lord picking up the same conversation with no break except the interchangeability of the terms for God.

The passage, however, that really clinches this remarkable identification is Exodus 23:20-23. There God promises to send his angel ahead of the children of Israel as they go through the desert. The Israelites were warned they must obey and not rebel against this angel. The reason was a stunning one: "Since my Name is in him." God would never share his memorial name with anyone else, for Isaiah 42:8 advised that he would never share his glory with another. Thus the name of God stands for himself. And when a person is said to have the name of God in him, that person is God!

This angel has divine qualities, prerogatives and authority. He has the power to give life (Gen 16:10) and to see and know all (Gen 16:13; Ex 3:7). Only God can forgive sin, yet this angel did the same in Exodus 23:21. The angel performed miracles such as keeping a burning bush from being consumed (Ex 3:2), smiting Egypt with plagues (Ex 3:20), calling forth fire on the rock to consume the meal set for him (Judg 6:21) and ascending the flame of the altar (Judg 13:20).

Finally, this angel commanded and received worship from Moses (Ex 3:5) and Joshua (Josh 5:14). Angels were not to receive worship in either testament. When John attempted to worship an angel in Revelation 19:10; 22:8-9, he was corrected quickly and told not to do it.

It is clear from this abundance of evidence that the angel of the Lord in the Old Testament was a pre-incarnate form of our Lord Jesus Christ who would later permanently take on flesh when he came as a babe in Bethlehem. But mark it well: the one who came after John, had already been before—he was that angel of the Lord. His full deity was always observed and yet he presented the same mystery of the Trinity that would later be observed in "I and the Father are one" (Jn 10:30) and "my other witness is the Father, who sent me" (Jn 8:18). It is that word *sent* that ties together the angel, messenger or sent one into an Old Testament theology of Christophanies, appearances of God in human form.

· CHAPTER 26 ·

Jephthah Did
with Her as
He Had Vowed

*And Jephthah made a vow to the LORD: "If you give the
Ammonites into my hands, whatever comes out of the door of my
house to meet me when I return in triumph from the Ammonites
will be the LORD's, and I will sacrifice it as a burnt
offering." . . . When Jephthah returned to his house in Mizpah,
who should come out to meet him but his daughter. . . .
She was an only child. . . . When he saw her, he tore his
clothes and cried, "Oh! My daughter! You have made me miserable
and wretched, because I have made a vow to the LORD
that I cannot break." And he did to her as he had vowed.*
JUDGES 11:30-31, 34-35, 39

The story of Jephthah and his famous vow, has caused heated debates
among interpreters. The question dividing interpreters is simply,
Did Jephthah sacrifice his own daughter—or did he not? If he did,
did God condone such an unspeakable act?

Almost all earlier commentators and writers on Israel's history
portrayed Jephthah as actually offering up his own daughter. It
was not until the Middle Ages that commentators began to look
for ways to soften Jephthah's roguishness. Indeed, sane men and

women would naturally be incensed and shocked by Jephthah's autocratic and nonbiblical ways of thinking and acting.

But the reader must remember the theme of Judges: Everyone was doing what was right in his or her own eyes. Jephthah was no different. As a matter of fact, the people hesitated to call him as judge over the tribes on the east bank (before he was finally named) because his mother was a prostitute and his own brothers had driven him from the family inheritance.

There are three main questions to answer here: (1) Exactly what did Jephthah mean by his vow? (2) How did he carry it out? (3) Did God condone his actions? All else, as they say in Jewish circles, is commentary.

Before Jephthah marched out of Mizpah, he solemnly vowed to give God whoever came out the door of his house if he returned victorious over the Ammonites. This raises the issue of vows and the problem translating *whoever*.

Vows are not unbiblical, but there are some dangers to avoid in making them. First, it is best to avoid making vows that will afterwards prove difficult for one's conscience or ability to carry out (Prov 20:25; Eccles 5:2-6). Second, vows should never be used to purchase favor with God—as if we could work for God's grace or we could influence God to do for us what he would not otherwise do. Instead, our vows should express gratitude to him for his unmerited favor.

But when a vow has been made, the promise ought to be fulfilled (Num 36:2-13; Ps 15:4; 66:14; 76:11; Acts 5:1-4). Oaths or vows which violate a moral law of God, however, should not be kept. Therefore, the rash promise of Herod, which resulted in the request of John the Baptist's head, should never have been kept. Unfortunately, it was (Mk 6:23-27). Here, Herod should have retreated from his vow and sought pardon from all involved for making it at all. Only vows and oaths made in faith need never be regretted. Others will be the occasion of lament or shock.

What then did Jephthah vow? Some have tried to soften the vow by translating what was vowed as *whatever comes out*. However, if the Hebrew text intended this neuter idea (which would have allowed for anything including Jephthah's animals), it should have used a different gender here (neuter in the Hebrew would have been signalled by the feminine form of the word). Since the masculine form is used, and the verb is *to come out*, it must refer (as it does in every other context) only to persons and not to animals or anything else.

Jephthah promised that whoever first came out to meet him on his victorious return would belong to the Lord and be sacrificed to the Lord. Did he mean this literally? If he did not, then why did he use these words? And if he did, then how could a judge, with his unusual anointing of the Holy Spirit for the task of leadership in battle, be guilty of such a gross violation of an explicit law of God (Lev 18:21; Deut 12:31)—the injunction against human sacrifice?

Such irrational behavior can only be explained in this manner: God's approval of a person in one area is no guarantee of approval in all areas of life. For example, David was also Spirit-led and a man after God's own heart, but not everything David did should be imitated by all Spirit-led believers.

Some interpreters have attempted to translate the word *and* between *will be the Lord's* and *I will sacrifice* as a disjunctive use of the Hebrew *and* meaning here *or*. Unfortunately for this ingenious solution (and it would be that), this translation of the Hebrew particle is never permitted anywhere else in the Old Testament. The only other case where it has been tried (2 Kings 18:27) also appears to be very questionable.

Jephthah was acquainted with the law of Moses which forbade human sacrifice. Judges 11:12-28 shows he knew the history of Israel and could recite it at will. But this, of course, is no proof that what he *knew* he always *did*, any more than our knowing what is right guarantees we will always do it.

That Jephthah actually sacrificed his daughter, tragic as that would be, seems the most natural reading of the text. If Jephthah's "sacrifice" of his daughter meant relegating her to a life of perpetual virginity and service at the temple, not one word in the text says so. The only possible support is the comment that whoever comes out of the house "will be the Lord's" (v. 31). But the statement immediately after this proves he had a whole burnt offering in mind—"sacrifice . . . as a burnt offering."

There is one other problem with the dedication to the temple view. Why didn't Jephthah pay the monetary substitute set forth in Leviticus 27:1-8 in order to gain the release of his daughter? After all, it bothered him that she would be childless and his line and name would fall out of the rosters of Israel. A woman could be redeemed for thirty shekels of silver (Lev 27:4), if need be.

Some, like James Jordan, attempt to answer this critically important question by quoting Leviticus 27:28-29 which demands that any person who has been "devoted" to the Lord may not be ransomed. This is true, but the term used there for *devoted* is a very technical term. It is the opposite of a voluntary offering, which is the essence of a vow. In the conquest, Jericho was such a "devoted" place to the Lord, and therefore everything in that town belonged to God. What could not be burned, such as silver, gold or iron, had to be collected and placed in the tabernacle. Thus when Achan took some of the loot of Jericho for himself, he stole from God. (For a more extensive explanation, see chapter twenty-seven.)

But that is not what we are talking about here. Jephthah was not forced to "devote" his daughter for destruction in return for God's victory over the Ammonites. He did it voluntarily and thus these verses do not apply. Furthermore, persons devoted under that "ban" *(herem)* were slain, not as a sacrifice or a burnt offering, but as required by the command of God (Num 21:2-3; Deut 13:12-18; 1 Sam 15:33). The irony of this whole situation is, as Micah warns us, that a person cannot offer the "fruit of [his or her] body [in exchange] for the sin of [his or her] soul" (Mic 6:6-8).

Why does the text note in verse 39 that "she was a virgin" if Jephthah actually sacrificed her? The answer is that the Hebrew is best translated as a pluperfect, "She had never known a man." This point is added to emphasize the tragedy and grief of the events described.

If Jephthah's daughter was immolated, in contradiction to every decent theocratic teaching of the Mosaic law, why would her decease be the occasion for an annual celebration or memorial in Holy Writ? Would not the people in revulsion have silently tried to forget it as best they could?

The fact that the "young women of Israel go out for four days to commemorate the daughter of Jephthah the Gileadite" (Judg 11:40) is not a biblical endorsement of this event. Nor does it say this event was observed throughout all Israel. But even if it were a national holiday, it came about by local or national custom and not by the word of God from his prophets or inspired leaders.

The tragedy of Jephthah's foolish and autocratic vow stands as a reminder to the perverseness of human wisdom when we fail to depend on the living God. In no way should we make Jephthah's action normative for other believers who also have made foolish vows in the past and feel that now they must stick to their guns, as it were, because the Bible says Jephthah stuck to his vow. Just because something is described in Scripture does not mean God prescribes us to follow it. Only a direct word from God based in his character or authority can have that claim over our lives.

CHAPTER 27

Go and Completely Destroy the Amalekites

*And he sent you on a mission, saying, "Go
and completely destroy those wicked
people, the Amalekites; make war
on them until you have wiped them out."*
1 SAMUEL 15:18

A chief objection to the view that the God of the Old Testament is a God of love and mercy is the divine command to exterminate all men, women and children belonging to the seven or eight Canaanite nations. How, ask most serious readers of the text, could God approve of blanket condemnations, of the genocide of an entire group of people?

Attempts to tone down the command or to mitigate its stark reality will fail from the start. God's instructions are too clear, and too many texts speak of consigning whole populations to divine destruction: Exodus 23:32-33; 34:11-16; and Deuteronomy 7:1-5; 20:16-18.

In most of these situations, a distinctive Old Testament concept known as *herem* is present. It means "curse," "that which stood under the ban" or "that which was dedicated to destruction." The root idea of this term was "separation"; however, this situation was not the positive concept of sanctification in which someone or something was set aside for service and the glory of God. This was the opposite side of the same coin: to set aside or separate for destruction.

God dedicated these things or persons to destruction because they violently and steadfastly impeded or opposed his work over a long period of time. This "dedication to destruction" was not used frequently in the Old Testament. It was reserved for the spoils of Southern Canaan (Num 21:2-3), Jericho (Josh 6:21), Ai (Josh 8:26), Makedah (Josh 10:28) and Hazor (Josh 11:11).

Long and unabated toleration of idolaters in a city or nation ultimately anathematized those ignoring natural revelation of God, as well as knowledge of God occasionally coming from other evidence (Deut 13:12-15). Their treatment was set forth in Deuteronomy 7:2-6.

In a most amazing prediction, Abraham was told that his descendants would be exiled and mistreated for four hundred years (in rounded-off numbers for 430 years) before God would lead them out of that country. The reason for so long a delay, Genesis 15:13-16 explains, is that "the sin of the Amorites [the Canaanites] has not yet reached its full measure." Thus, God waited for centuries while the Amalekites and those other Canaanite groups slowly filled up their own cups of destruction by their sinful behavior. God never acted precipitously against them; his grace and mercy waited to see if they would repent and turn from their headlong plummet into self-destruction.

Not that the conquering Israelites were without sin. Deuteronomy 9:5 makes it clear that to the Israelites: "It is not because of your righteousness or your integrity that you are going in to

take possession of their land; but on account of the wickedness
of these nations."

These nations were cut off to prevent the corruption of Israel
and the rest of the world (Deut 20:16-18). When a nation starts
burning children as a gift to the gods (Lev 18:21) and practices
sodomy, bestiality and all sorts of loathsome vices (Lev 18:25, 27-
30), the day of God's grace and mercy has begun to run out.

Just as a surgeon does not hesitate to amputate a gangrenous
limb, even if he cannot help cutting off some healthy flesh, so
God must do the same. This is not doing evil that good may
come; it is removing the cancer that could infect all of society and
eventually destroy the remaining good.

God could have used pestilence, hurricanes, famine, diseases or
anything else he wanted. In this case he chose to use Israel to
reveal his power, but the charge of cruelty against God is no
more deserved in this case than it is in the general order of things
in the world where all of these same calamities happen.

In the providential acts of life, it is understood that individuals
share in the life of their families and nations. As a result, we as
individuals participate both in the families' and nations' rewards
as well as its punishments. Naturally, this will involve some, so
called, innocent people; however, even that argument involves us
in a claim to omniscience which we do not possess. If the women
and children were spared in those profane Canaanite nations,
how long would it be before a fresh crop of adults would emerge
just like their pagan predecessors?

Why was God so dead set against the Amalekites? When the
Israelites were struggling through the desert toward Canaan, the
Amalekites picked off the weak, sick and elderly at the end of the
line of march and brutally murdered these stragglers. Warned
Moses, "Remember what the Amalekites did to you along the
way when you came out of Egypt. When you were weary and
worn out, they met you on your journey and cut off all who were

lagging behind; they had no fear of God" (Deut 25:17-18).

Some commentators note that the Amalekites were not merely plundering or disputing who owned what territories; they were attacking God's chosen people to discredit the living God. Some trace the Amalekites' adamant hostility all through the Old Testament, including the most savage butchery of all in Haman's proclamation that all Jews throughout the Persian empire could be massacred on a certain day (Esther 3:8-11). Many make a case that Haman was an Amalekite. His actions then would ultimately reveal this nation's deep hatred for God, manifested toward the people through whom God had chosen to bless the whole world.

· CHAPTER 28 ·

To Obey Is Better Than Sacrifice

*But Samuel said, "What then is this bleating of sheep in
my ears? What is this lowing of cattle that I hear?" Saul
answered, "The soldiers brought them from the Amalekites; they
spared the best of the sheep and cattle to sacrifice to the LORD
your God, but we totally destroyed the rest." . . .
But Samuel replied: "Does the LORD delight in burnt offerings
and sacrifices as much as in obeying the voice of
the LORD? To obey is better than sacrifice, and to heed
is better than the fat of rams."*
1 SAMUEL 15:14-15, 22

This passage and a few other texts appear to repudiate all sacrifices.
Though some texts call for burnt offerings or daily offerings to
God (for example, Ex 29:18, 36; Lev 1—7), others appear to dis-
parage any sacrifices, even as our text in 1 Samuel 15:22 seems
to do. How do we reconcile this seeming contradiction?

God derives very little satisfaction from the external act of
sacrificing. In fact, he complains, "I have no need of a bull from
your stall or of goats from your pens. . . . If I were hungry I

would not tell you, for the world is mine, and all that is in it" (Ps 50:9, 12).

Indeed, David learned this same lesson the hard way. After his sin with Bathsheba and the rebuke of Nathan the prophet, David confessed, "The sacrifices of God are a broken spirit; a broken and contrite heart, O God, you will not despise" (Ps 51:17). After the priority of the heart attitude had been corrected, it was possible for David to go on to say, "Then there will be righteous sacrifices, whole burnt offerings to delight you; then bulls will be offered on your altar" (Ps 51:19).

Samuel's harangue seconds the message of the writing prophets: Perfunctory acts of worship and ritual, apart from diligent obedience, were basically worthless to God and the individual.

This is why the prophet Isaiah stormily rebuked his nation for their empty ritualism. What good, he lamented, were all the sacrifices, New Moon festivals, sabbaths, convocations, and filing into the temple of God? So worthless was all this feverish activity that God said he was fed up with it all (Is 1:11-15). What was needed, instead, was a whole new heart attitude as the proper preparation for meeting God. Warned Isaiah, " 'Wash and make yourselves clean. . . . Come now, let us reason together,' says the LORD. 'Though your sins are like scarlet, they shall be as white as snow; though they are red as crimson, they shall be like wool' " (Is 1:16, 18). Then real sacrifices could be offered to God.

Jeremiah records the same complaint: "Your burnt offerings are not acceptable; your sacrifices do not please me" (Jer 6:20). So deceptive was the nation's trust in this hollow worship that Jeremiah later announced that God had wanted more than sacrifices when he brought Israel out of Egypt (Jer 7:22). He had wanted the people to trust him. It was always tempting to substitute attendance at God's house, heartless worship or possessing God's Word for active response to that Word (Jer 7:9-15, 21-

26; 8:8-12).

No less definitive were the messages of Hosea (Hos 6:6) and Micah (Mic 6:6-8). The temptation to externalize religion and to use it only in emergency situations was altogether too familiar.

Samuel's rebuke belongs to the same class of complaints. It was couched in poetry as some of those listed above were. It also had a proverbial form. Thus its absolute moral truth must be understood comparatively, even though the full form was not always stated that way. The proverb was stated in terms that call for setting priorities. Accordingly, one must read an implied, "This first and then that." These "better" wisdom sayings, of course, directly point to such a priority. What does *not* follow is that what is denied, or not called "better," is thereby rejected by God. That is not true. Arguing on those grounds would ignore the statement's proverbial structure.

God does approve of sacrificing, but he does not wish to have it at the expense of full obedience to his Word or as a substitute for a personal relationship of love and trust. Sacrifices, however, were under the Old Testament economy. Animal sacrifices are no longer necessary today, because Christ was our sacrifice, once for all (Heb 10:1-18). Nevertheless, the principle remains the same: What use is performing outward acts of religion with all of its paraphernalia if that religious activity is not grounded in an obedient heart of faith? True religious affection for God begins in the heart and not in acts of worship or the accompanying vestments and ritual!

· C H A P T E R 2 9 ·

God Does Not Lie or Change His Mind

*He who is the Glory of Israel does
not lie or change his mind; for
he is not a man, that he
should change his mind.*
1 SAMUEL 15:29

Here in 1 Samuel 15 we have a clear statement about God's truthfulness and unchanging character. But elsewhere in the Old Testament we read of God repenting or changing his mind. Does God change his mind? If so, does that discredit his truthfulness or his unchanging character? If not, what do these other Old Testament texts mean?

It can be affirmed from the start that God's essence and character, his resolute determination to punish sin and to reward virtue are unchanging (see Mal 3:6). These are absolute and unconditional affirmations which Scripture everywhere teaches.

But this does not mean that all his promises and warnings are unconditional. Many turn on either an expressed or an implied condition.

The classic example of this conditional teaching is Jeremiah 18:7-10. "If at any time I announce that a nation or kingdom is to be uprooted, torn down and destroyed, and if that nation I warned repents of its evil, then I will relent and not inflict on it the disaster I had planned. And if at another time I announce that a nation or kingdom is to be built up and planted, and if it does evil in my sight and does not obey me, then I will reconsider the good I had intended to do for it."

This principle clearly states the condition underlying most of God's promises and threats even when it is not made explicit, as in the case of Jonah. Therefore, whenever God does not fulfill a promise or execute a threat that he has made, the explanation is obvious: in all of these cases, the change has not come in God, but in the individual or nation.

Of course some of God's promises are unconditional for they rest solely on his mercy and grace. These would be: his covenant with the seasons after Noah's flood (Gen 8:22); his promise of salvation in the oft-repeated covenant to Abraham, Isaac, Jacob and David; his promise of the New Covenant; and his promise of the New Heaven and the New Earth.

What, then, was the nature of the change in God that 1 Samuel 15:11 talks about, when he says, "I am grieved that I have made Saul king, because he has turned away from me and has not carried out my instructions"? If God is unchangeable, why did he "repent" or "grieve over" the fact that he had made Saul king?

God is not a frozen automaton who cannot respond to persons; he is a living person who can and does react to others as much, and more genuinely, than we do to each other. Thus the same word *repent*, is used for two different concepts both in this passage and elsewhere in the Bible. One shows his responsiveness to individuals and the other shows his steadfastness to himself and to his thoughts and designs.

Thus the text affirms that God changed his actions toward Saul in order to remain true to his own character or essence. Repentance in God is not, as it is in us, an evidence of indecisiveness. It is rather a change in his method of responding to another person based on some change in the other individual. The change, then, was in Saul. The problem was in Saul's partial obedience, his wayward heart and covetousness.

While God repented that he had given Saul the kingdom along with its honor and power, he did not repent giving him wisdom and grace or his fear and love; indeed, the gifts and callings of God are without repentance.

To assert that God is unchanging does not mean he cannot experience regret, grief and repentance. If unchangeableness meant transcendent detachment from people and events, God would pay an awful price for immutability. Instead, God enters into a relationship with mortal beings that demonstrates his willingness to respond to each person's action within the ethical sphere of their obedience to his will.

When our sin or repentance change our relationship with God, his changing responses to us no more affect his essential happiness or blessedness than Christ's deity affects his ability genuinely to suffer on the cross for our sin.

CHAPTER 30

Uzzah Reached for the Ark and God Struck Him

When they came to the threshing floor of Nacon,
Uzzah reached out and took hold of the ark of God,
because the oxen stumbled. The LORD's anger burned
against Uzzah because of his irreverent act;
therefore God struck him down and he died there
beside the ark of God.
2 SAMUEL 6:6-7

Over the years many have complained that God was unfair to kill Uzzah when he involuntarily tried to protect the ark of God from damage or shame when the oxen stumbled and the ark slipped. Should not Uzzah have been praised for lunging forward to protect the ark of God?

There is no doubt that David's intentions were noble and good in bringing the ark to Jerusalem. Now that his kingdom was established, he did not forget his earlier vow to return the ark to its rightful place of prominence. But what began as a joyful day quickly became a day of national grief and shame. Why?

A significant omission in the first three verses of 2 Samuel 6 sets the scene for failure. Previously when David needed counsel, for example when he was attacked by the Philistines, the text records that David "inquired of the Lord" (2 Sam 5:19, 23). But those words are sadly missing in 2 Samuel 6:1-3. Instead, we are told in the parallel account in 1 Chronicles 13:1-3 that David "conferred with each of his officers."

There was no need to consult these men. God had already given clear instructions in Numbers 4:5-6 as to how to move the ark. It should be covered with a veil, to shield the holiness of God from any kind of rash intrusion, and then carried on poles on the shoulders of the Levites (Num 7:9).

God had plainly revealed his will, but David had a better idea— one he had learned from the pagan Philistines. He would put it on a "new cart" (2 Sam 6:3). However, God had never said anything about using a new cart. This was a human invention contrary to the will and law of God.

Thus David did things in the wrong way, following his own ideas or those of others instead of God's ways. Surely this passage warns that it is not enough to have a worthy purpose and a proper spirit when we enter into the service of God; God's work must also be performed in God's way. Pursuing the right end does not automatically imply using the right means.

But why did God's anger break out against Uzzah if David was at fault? The Lord had plainly taught that even the Kohathites, the Levite family designated to carry the ark, "must not touch the holy things or they will die" (Num 4:15). Even if Uzzah were not a Kohathite or even a Levite, he still would know what the law taught in Numbers 4 and 7. God not only keeps his promises, but he also fulfills his threats!

When the Philistines, who had no access to the special revelation of God, sinned by touching the ark and using a new cart to transport it, God's anger did not burn against them (1 Sam 6). Therefore, God is more merciful toward those less knowledge-

able of his will than toward those who are. This is why it will
be more tolerable for Sodom and Gomorrah in the day of Judgment than it will be for those who personally witnessed the great
acts of the Savior in Capernaum (Mt 11:23-24).

Uzzah's motive, like David's, was pure; but he disregarded the
written Word of God, just as David did. Thus one sin led to
another. Consulting one's peers is no substitute for obeying God
when he has spoken. Good intentions, with unsanctified minds,
interfere with the kingdom of God. This is especially true of the
worship of God and the concept of his holiness.

Because God is holy, he is free of all moral imperfections. To
help mortals understand this better, a sharp line of demarcation
was drawn between holy things and the common or profane.
Our word *profane* means "before" or "forth from the temple."
Thus all that was apart from the temple, where the holiness of
God was linked, was by definition profane. However, Uzzah's act
made the holiness associated with the ark also profane and thereby brought disrepute to God as well.

It is unthinkable that God could condone a confusion or a
diffusion of the sacred and the profane. To take something holy
and inject into it the realm of the profane was to confuse the
orders of God. This is why God burned Nadab and Abihu when
they offered to the Lord what he had not prescribed and in ways
and times which violated his holiness (Lev 10:2). Likewise in 1
Samuel 6:19, seventy men of Beth Shemesh were killed for peer-
ing into the ark. The profane is not only in opposition to the
holiness of God; it confuses the secular and the sacred.

Finally, Jeremiah 25:6 warns, "Do not provoke me to anger.
. . . Then I will not harm you." And the same could be said for
David's response to God's action: "My son, do not make light of
[or despise] the Lord's discipline" (Heb 12:5). Obedience is pref-
erable to learning that God and his Word remain true when we
insist on being foolish.

· CHAPTER 31 ·

The Lord Sends a Lying Spirit

> And the LORD said, "Who will entice Ahab into attacking
> Ramoth Gilead and going to his death there?" One suggested
> this, and another that. Finally, a spirit came forward,
> stood before the LORD and said, "I will entice him." "By
> what means?" the LORD asked. "I will go out and be a lying
> spirit in the mouths of all his prophets," he said. "You will
> succeed in enticing him," said the LORD. "Go and do it."
>
> 1 KINGS 22:20-22

Could the God of truth be guilty of sponsoring or condoning falsehood?
Some have charged just that. The passages that are raised to back
this charge are 1 Kings 22:20-23, Jeremiah 4:10 and Ezekiel 14:9.

Such a charge is possible only if one forgets that many biblical
writers dismiss secondary causes and attribute all that happens
directly to God, since he is over all things. Therefore, statements
expressed in the imperative form of the verb often represent
only what is permitted to happen. Accordingly, when the devils
begged Jesus to let them enter the swine, he said, "Go" (Mt 8:31).
This did not make him the active sponsor of evil; he merely
permitted the demons to do what they wanted to do. In a similar

manner, Jesus commanded Judas, "What you are about to do, do quickly" (Jn 13:27). But Jesus did not become the author of the evil perpetrated on himself.

God can be described as deceiving Ahab only because the biblical writer does not discriminate between what someone does and what he permits. It is true, of course, that in 1 Kings 22 God seems to do more than permit the deception. Without saying that God does evil that good may come, we can say that God overrules the full tendencies of pre-existing evil so that the evil promotes God's eternal plan, contrary to its own tendency and goals.

Because Ahab had abandoned the Lord his God and hardened his own heart, God allowed his ruin by the very instrument Ahab had sought to prostitute for his own purposes, namely, prophecy. God used the false declarations of the false prophets that Ahab was so enamored with as his instruments of judgment the same way he might use a heathen nation to chastise Israel (that is to say, his use of Assyria in punishing Israel, Is 10:5; or his use of Babylon for similar reasons, Hab 1:2-11).

That God was able to overrule the evil and guile to which Ahab was so susceptible does not excuse the guilty prophets or their gullible listener. Even though the lying spirit had the Lord's permission, this did not excuse the prophets who misused their gifts. They fed the king exactly what he wanted to hear. Their words were nothing less than echoes of the king's desires. Thus both the lying prophets, the king and Israel were equally culpable before God. The responsibility had to be shared. These prophets spoke "out of their own minds."

This principle is further confirmed when we note that the passage in question is a vision that Micaiah *reveals to Ahab*. God is telling Ahab, "Wise up. I am allowing your prophets to lie to you." In a sense, God is revealing further truth to Ahab rather than lying to him. If God were truly trying to entrap Ahab into a life-threatening situation, he would not have revealed the plan

to Ahab! Even so, Ahab refuses to heed God's truth and follows
his prophets' advice anyway.

The other two passages used to charge God with falsehood are
easier to understand. In Ezekiel 14:9 we have another case of
God allowing spiritual blindness to take its course. The biblical
writer merely attributes the whole process of hardening of heart
followed by judgment as falling within God's sovereignty. The
strong statements of Jeremiah 4:10 and 20:7 are merely complaints of the prophet who had mistaken the promise of God's
presence for the insurance that no evil or derision would come
on him or his ministry. However, these verses cannot be cited
as the basis for giving any credence to the charge that God is
deceptive.

• C H A P T E R 3 2 •

Two Bears Mauled Forty-Two Youths

From there Elisha went up to Bethel. As he was walking along the road, some youths came out of the town and jeered at him. "Go on up, you baldhead!" they said. "Go on up, you baldhead!" He turned around, looked at them and called down a curse on them in the name of the LORD. Then two bears came out of the woods and mauled forty-two of the youths.
2 KINGS 2:23-24

Lhe way many read this text, a mild personal offense by some innocent little children was turned into a federal case by a crotchety old prophet as short on hair as he was on humor. Such unfavorable assessments of this incident on the road up to Bethel have brought more criticism of the Bible than almost any other narrative. Put in its sharpest form, the complaint goes: How can I believe in a God who would send bears to devour toddlers for innocently teasing an old man whose appearance probably was unusual even for that day?

At first reading, it appears the prophet chanced on guileless children merrily playing on the outskirts of Bethel. Seeing this strange-looking man, they began to chant in merriment, "Go on up, you baldhead! Go on up, you baldhead!" Instead of viewing the situation for what it was, the old prophet became enraged (as some would tell the story), whirled around, and, with eyes flashing anger, shouted a curse in the name of the Lord.

But this is a false reconstruction of the event. The problem begins with the two Hebrew words for *little children*, as many older translations term the youths. If we are to untangle this puzzling incident, the age and accountability level of these children must take first priority. *Little children* is an unfortunate translation. The Hebrew expression *qetanaim na'arim* is best rendered *young lads* or *young men*. From numerous examples where ages are specified in the Old Testament, we know that these were boys from twelve to thirty years old. One of these words described Isaac at his sacrifice in Genesis 22:12, when Isaac was easily in his early twenties. It described Joseph in Genesis 37:2 when he was seventeen years of old. In fact, the same word described army men in 1 Kings 20:14-15.

If someone objects, yes, but the word *qetanaim* [which is translated *little* in some versions] makes the difference in this context, we will answer that it is best translated *younger*, not *little*. Furthermore, these words have a good deal of elasticity to them. For example, Samuel asked Jesse, "Are these all your children [*na'arim*]?" But Jesse replied, "There is still the youngest [*qatan*]." Thus David, who was the "youngest child," according to the older translations, was old enough to keep sheep and fight a giant soon after (1 Sam 16:11-12).

Little children, then, does not mean toddlers or even elementary-school-aged youngsters; these are men or young men whose ages vary between twelve and thirty!

But was Elisha an old man short on patience and a sense of humor? This charge is also distorted, for Elisha can hardly have been more than twenty-five when this incident happened. He

lived nearly sixty years after this incident, since it came, we
would judge, shortly after Elijah's translation into heaven. Some
would place Elijah's translation around 860 B.C. and Elisha's
death around 795 B.C. While Elijah's ministry had lasted less
than a decade, Elisha's extended at least fifty-five years, through
the reigns of Jehoram, Jehu, Jehoahaz and Joash.

Did Elisha lose his temper? What was so wrong in calling him
a "baldhead" even if he might not have been bald, being less than
thirty?

The word *baldhead* was a term of scorn in the Old Testament
(Is 3:17, 24). Natural baldness was very rare in the ancient Near
East. So scarce was baldness that it carried with it a suspicion of
leprosy.

Whether Elisha was prematurely bald or not, it is clear that the
epithet was used in utter contempt, as a word of insult marking
him as despicable.

But since it is highly improbable that Elisha was prematurely
bald, the insult was aimed not so much at the prophet, but at the
God who had sent him. The point is clear from the other phrase.
"Go on up," they clamored. "Go on up!" These were not topo-
graphical references to the uphill grade of the Bethel road. Instead, the youths were alluding to Elijah's translation to heaven.
This they did not believe or acknowledge as God's work in their
midst. To put it in modern terms, they jeered, "Blast off! Blast
off! You go too. Get out of here. We are tired of both of you."
These Bethel ruffians used the same Hebrew verb that this second chapter of 2 Kings began with to describe the taking up of
Elijah into heaven. The connection cannot be missed.

Apparently, news of Elijah's ascension to glory traveled near
and far but was greeted with contemptuous disbelief by many,
including this youthful mob. The attack was on God, not his
prophet.

Elisha uses no profanity in placing a curse on these young men.

He merely cited the law of God which the inhabitants of Bethel knew well. Moses had taught, "If you remain hostile toward me and refuse to listen to me. . . . I will send wild animals against you, and they will rob you of your children" (Lev 26:21-22).

Elisha did not abuse these young men nor did he revile them; he was content to leave the work of judging to God. He pronounced a judgment on them and asked God to carry out the action which he had promised when his name, his cause and his word were under attack. No doubt these young men only reflected what they heard at the dinner table each evening as the population went further and further away from God.

The savagery of wild animals was brutal enough, but it was mild compared to the legendary cruelty of the Assyrians who would appear to complete God's judgment in 722 B.C. The disastrous Fall of Samaria would have been avoided had the people repented after the bear attack and the increasingly severe divine judgments that followed it. But instead of turning back to God, Israel, as would Judah in a later day, "mocked God's messengers, despised his words and scoffed at his prophets until the wrath of the LORD was aroused against his people and there was no remedy" (2 Chron 36:16).

Instead of demonstrating unleashed cruelty, the bear attack shows God trying repeatedly to bring his people back to himself through smaller judgments until the people's sin is too great and judgment must come full force.

· C H A P T E R   3 3 ·

Nevertheless, the Lord Did Not Turn Away from His Fierce Anger

*Nevertheless, the LORD did not turn away
from the heat of his fierce anger,
which burned against Judah because of all
that Manasseh had done to provoke him to anger.*
2 KINGS 23:26

Is it possible to overcome the effects of years of wickedness and evil by a time of unprecedented reform and revival? Can a godly grandson's thirty-year reign make up for his ruthless grandfather and father who provoked God to the limit for sixty years? In other words, does evil have a corporate and cumulative effect on society, or as the saying goes, "Does every tub always stand on its own bottom?"

In spite of the probability that King Manasseh of Judah became king, or co-regent, about ten years before his father, King Hezekiah, died, his godly father had no influence on this rebellious son's fifty-year reign. This is especially shocking after the great revival under Hezekiah.

Manasseh illustrates the old saying, "God may have children, but he has no grandchildren." In his case, a cultured, godly home was no guarantee that he would follow the Lord.

Therefore, for half a century Manasseh duplicated all the depravity of the Canaanites. He murdered so many righteous men that there were too few to defend Jerusalem when the need arose (2 Kings 21:10-15); all of which the people tolerated. This ruthless monarch ordered Isaiah "sawed in two" (Heb 11:37). Manasseh's idolatry and unrighteousness brought Judah and Jerusalem to the unavoidable rejection by God (2 Kings 24:3; Jer 15:4).

Manasseh did have what is today called a deathbed conversion experience. For offending the Assyrian king Ashurbanipal, Manasseh was hauled off to prison where "in his distress he sought the favor of the LORD his God and humbled himself greatly before the God of his fathers. And when he prayed to him, the LORD was moved by his entreaty and listened to his plea. . . . Then Manasseh knew that the LORD is God" (2 Chron 33:12-13). This came at the end of his reign.

However, it was too late to reverse the trends in society and his own household. Manasseh was succeeded by his wicked son Amon, who himself was assassinated by other ruffians. 2 Chronicles 33:23 pointedly informs us that King Amon "did not humble himself before the LORD."

Mercifully God prepared Amon's eight-year-old son, Josiah, to take over as king. From the very beginning, Josiah walked in David's ways and not in the ways of his grandfather Manasseh or his father, Amon. He deserves the credit for initiating one of the most intensive periods of reformation and revival known in Judah's history.

Indeed, with the chance finding of the Book of the Law, which had been lost and unknown for years, Josiah inaugurated a magnificent revival. It seems this revival never penetrated the culture, for it carried no lasting effects and had insufficient strength to overcome the years of compounded evil accumulated under Manasseh.

Hence the hard saying of our text has special meaning. Josiah's marvelous reformation and revival was not sufficient to offset the evil done by his father and grandfather before him.

Though Josiah ended outward and gross forms of idolatry in his sincere desire to dedicate himself and his people to the Lord, the people themselves did not turn back to the Lord. The people followed their religious king out of fear, but their hearts and minds, apparently, were affected very little.

If the early chapters of Jeremiah reflect the conditions under King Josiah, then they describe the people's deep inner apostasy, not only before Josiah's reform and discovery of the Book of the Law, but also during it and following it.

The Holy One of Israel could no longer forgive and extend mercy; he at last was obligated to bring the judgment foretold to Manasseh in 2 Kings 21:12-15. Thus, even though God is patient and long-suffering in his mercy, judgment will and must eventually come, even though someone arrives on the scene who seemingly cancels the debt standing against all the people.

CHAPTER 34

Satan Incited David to Take a Census of Israel

*Satan rose up against Israel and
incited David to take a
census of Israel.*
1 CHRONICLES 21:1

*Again the anger of the LORD burned against
Israel, and he incited David against them,
saying, "Go and take a census of Israel and Judah."*
2 SAMUEL 24:1

Why was a census a sin? Had not God commanded Moses twice
to take a census in Numbers 1 and 26? Yet in 2 Samuel, David
numbers Israel because God, angry with Israel, incites him to it;
1 Chronicles attributes the result to the influence of Satan on
David. Are these contradictory passages an instance where error
has crept into Scripture?

Let us first establish why census-taking could be sinful. In
effect, the census acted as a draft notice or a mustering of the
troops. Some conclude, based on 1 Chronicles 27:23-24, that
David sinned by numbering those people under twenty years of

age—an illegal act. Others see the numbering as doubting God's promise that David's descendants would be as measureless as the sand and stars. The best solution is that it was motivated by presumption. God had given David no objective or reason to go out to battle. Only David's pride and ambition could have brought on such an act.

But the *and* beginning 1 Chronicles 21:1 in some translations seems to invite us to look at the conclusion of chapter 20. Verse 8 mentions that the giant's descendants were among those whom David and his men vanquished. The connection could be that David, flushed with his successes, grew too big in his own eyes and opened the door for Satan to successfully tempt him.

This brings us to the second difficulty of this hard saying: Was it God or Satan who tempted David to sin? Satan is mentioned infrequently in the Old Testament. He was introduced in Job 1—2 and in the post-exilic period in Zechariah 3:1. However, in both of these latter cases, the definite article is used; 1 Chronicles 21:1 does not use it. Even though the doctrine of the supernatural being named *Satan* was not well developed in the Old Testament, the appearance of Satan cannot be reduced to Persian dualism or one's adversary in general. Even in the Garden of Eden there exists a hostile presence called *the serpent*. What is new in this passage is the formalizing of his name as *the adversary or opposer*. But the activities of the serpent and Satan make it clear that they are the same person.

How then does this relatively unidentified but never-absent personage play a key role in one version of David's sin when God receives the dubious credit in another?

The thought that God instigates or impels sinners to do evil is incorrect. In no sense could God author what he disapproves of and makes his whole kingdom stand against. How, then, shall we understand 2 Samuel 24:1 where God seems to instigate something, which he will immediately label as sin?

God may and does occasionally impel sinners to reveal the wickedness of their hearts in deeds. God merely presents the opportunity and occasion for letting the evil desires of the heart manifest themselves outwardly. In this manner, sinners may see more quickly the evil which lies dormant in their hearts and motivates them to act counter to God's will.

It is also true, according to the Hebrew thinking, that whatever God permits he commits. By allowing this census-taking, God is viewed as having brought about the act. The Hebrews were not very concerned with determining secondary causes and properly attributing them to the exact cause. Under the divine providence everything ultimately was attributed to him; why not say he did it in the first place?

Since the number of variations here between Samuel and Chronicles are greater than usual and point to no clear rationale for emphasizing one set of facts over another, scholars suggest that Chronicles may represent the better and more dependable text tradition of the original Hebrew rather than that reflected in our English versions of Samuel.

Although we should not overestimate the textual variants between Samuel and Chronicles in this chapter, the as-yet-unpublished texts from Qumran's Dead Sea Scrolls indicate that some of its Samuel readings agree with readings previously found only in Chronicles. This would bring more harmony to the differences in our texts.

Almost all students of Scripture judge that Chronicles was composed during the exile or just after it. Therefore it likely was based on an earlier form of the Samuel narrative no doubt well known and widely used by then. Note the way that the writer of Chronicles linked his materials; it reflects a linkage explicitly made in 2 Samuel 24:1. There the writer of 2 Samuel 24:1 noted, "Again the anger of the LORD burned," a reference to 2 Samuel 21:1-14 which also had to do with atonement for guilt. Accordingly, even though the chronicler omitted the material in 2 Samuel 23—24, he had a literary precedent for linking the materials in 2 Samuel 21 and 24. The selection of a site for the temple in Jerusalem marked a fitting climax to this phase of David's activity.

Having shown that David did indeed sin and that Satan, not God, was to blame, that still leaves all Israel the victims of the plague God sent to punish the sin. Fortunately, David's subjects were as guilty as their king, according to 2 Samuel 24:1. Thus God dealt with all Israel through the act of the king who exemplified the national spirit of pride.

· CHAPTER 35 ·

Go Home,
for This Is the
Lord's Doing

But this word of the LORD came to Shemaiah the
man of God: "Say to Rehoboam son of Solomon king of
Judah and to all the Israelites in Judah and Benjamin,
'This is what the LORD says: Do not go up
to fight against your brothers. Go home, every
one of you, for this is my doing.' "
2 CHRONICLES 11:2-4

After the ten northern tribes had renounced their allegiance to King
Rehoboam, the son of Solomon, Rehoboam decided that he
would force these renegades to submit to his sovereignty and to
pay the taxes which were their reason for leaving. This would
have pitted brother against brother in open civil war.

But God sent his prophet Shemaiah to intervene. King Rehoboam was commanded in the Lord's name to abandon his attempt at a military solution. Shemaiah's surprising announcement seemed to oppose all God's previous promises. The
prophet's assurance that God had permitted the incident sealed
the revolt, but left us with a dilemma: How could the division of

a nation be God's doing if he had previously promised otherwise? Having David's glorious kingdom divided into ten northern tribes and two southern tribes seemed contrary to every provision that God had so graciously given from the time of the patriarchs on. That is what makes this passage a hard saying. How could God apparently aid a cause that contravened his plan for Israel?

The Lord approved the revolt, not as the author of evil or as the instigator of the rebellion but as the one who must chastise the house of David which had refused to walk in his ways. Solomon had flouted the will and law of God by taking scores of foreign wives. These wives, in turn, had turned him from the Lord and exposed him to divine anger.

Rehoboam had only increased the guilt of the house of David. The tribes were already overwhelmed by taxation and unsatisfying treatment of their complaints. They had demanded that the burdens Solomon had placed on them be lightened, not increased. Instead, Rehoboam exacerbated the situation by deciding to tax them further.

The ten northern tribes already disliked and resisted the theocratic rule of the house of David. While they correctly detected Rehoboam's wrong attitudes toward his responsibilities as king, Rehoboam's treatment did not justify their actions. They chiefly rebelled against the God who had selected the dynasty of David and the tribe of Judah as the royal tribe. Apparently, they felt such rule did not represent enough of their northern interests; the taxation issue was as good a reason as any for seceding (see 1 Kings 12:19-24).

Here we meet another passage where human freedom and divine sovereignty seem opposed. This phenomenon is especially prevalent in Chronicles. Once again we must note that the biblical writers did not always take time to spell out secondary causes; for what God permits, he is often said to do *directly* since he is ultimately in charge. What the North intended as a revolt against the South, and thereby against the plan of God, God used, first to punish the house of David for its sin and second to reveal the North's sinful tendencies and spiritual bankruptcy. This latter fact is underscored by the number of the northern priests and Levites who abandoned their pasture lands and property to come to Judah and Jerusalem. The northern King Jeroboam had rejected their priesthood! With them came all those who "set their hearts on seeking the LORD, the God of Israel" (2 Chron 11:16).

• CHAPTER 36 •

Josiah Refused to Listen to What Neco Said at God's Command

Josiah, however, would not turn away from him,
but disguised himself to engage him in battle.
He would not listen to what Neco had said
at God's command but went to fight
him on the plain of Megiddo.
2 CHRONICLES 35:22

Few incidents in the life of Israel and Judah are as sad as this episode. Rarely had one of the nation's monarchs so genuinely desired to serve God. Even as Josiah began his reign at the tender age of eight, he had purposed to walk in the ways of David and not in the ways of his evil father, Amon, and grandfather Manasseh.

It was Josiah who had started the great reforms in Judah. These were followed by discovery of the Book of the Law when the temple was cleaned in the eighteenth year of his reign, 621 B.C. When at age twenty-six Josiah first had the the law of God read to him, he tore his robes in grief and true repentance before God. Here was one of history's great men. His heart was responsive to God, and he did not hesitate to humble himself before God (2 Chron 34:27).

But in 609 B.C., when this king with all his potential for furthering the kingdom of God was only thirty-nine, he was struck down by one giant act of foolish disobedience.

In 2 Kings 23:25-38, the catastrophe is partially explained: Even though Josiah had followed the Lord with all his heart, soul and strength and had obeyed the Law of Moses so that there was no king like him, yet God did not turn from his great wrath against Judah. God would still destroy Judah because of King Manasseh's sins and the superficial repentance of the people (see chapter 33). Such an explanation softens the blow of the pending tragedy.

In the Chronicles account, however, no such didactic connection was included. Instead, Josiah's godly obedience alone introduces the tragic episode: "After all this, when Josiah had set the temple in order" (2 Chron 35:20). This would seem to stress that Josiah was devoted to the temple right up to the end of his life.

The scene for Josiah's end was now set. The Assyrian king Asshur-uballit had established a new capital at Carchemish in 610 B.C. The Egyptians were interested in helping the Assyrians, for they feared that the emerging fortunes of the Babylonians would upset the balance of power in the Near East. Thus, in the summer of 609 B.C. a great Egyptian army moved up the Palestinian coast to join the Assyrians in a great counteroffensive.

A phrase in 2 Kings 23:29 sometimes translated "Neco went up *against* the king of Assyria" is better translated as "Neco went up *on behalf of* the king of Assyria, to the river Euphrates." When translated accurately, this verse illuminates Josiah's reason for fighting Neco.

Josiah viewed Neco's advance as a menace to his own designs for a reunited Hebrew state. Josiah thought that any friend of the hated Assyrians must be his enemy. Therefore he boldly disregarded all prophetic warnings to the contrary and directly intervened in this international affair, trying to block the Egyptian army from joining the Assyrians.

Amazingly enough, in this case the prophetic warnings do not come from one of Israel's traditional prophets but from a pagan Pharaoh who warns Josiah to halt his attempt to meddle with his mission. Neco claims that "God has told me to hurry; so stop opposing God, who is with me, or he will destroy you" (2 Chron 35:21).

Then follow the mournful, yet amazing words of the inspired writer: "Josiah, however, would not turn away from him, but disguised himself to engage in battle. He would not listen to what Neco had said at God's command, but went to fight him on the plain of Megiddo. Archers shot King Josiah, and . . . he died" (2 Chron 35:22-24).

This is indeed one of the strangest statements in Scripture, which we would dismiss as Egyptian propaganda had not the inspired writer confirmed that God did use a pagan monarch to warn Josiah and assist the Assyrians.

God had spoken to pagan kings previously without implying that they had become a prophet of Israel or converted to worshiping the one true God (see Gen 12:17-20; 20:3-7; and Dan 4:1-3). The instrument was not the focal point of the prophecy; its content was. God had also previously spoken through the mouth of an ass (Num 22:28-31) and would later speak through a profane High Priest (Jn 11:51). But King Josiah did not perceive that God could use such an instrument as a Pharaoh.

In an act reminiscent of King Ahab, Josiah disguised himself and went into a battle he was not supposed to be in. The archer's arrow found its mark, and Josiah was carried away to die at thirty-nine years of age.

But the plan of God was still operating. Josiah, it had been prophesied by Huldah, would be gathered to his fathers and "buried in peace" (2 Chron 34:28). His "eyes [would] not see all the disaster [God was] going to bring on [that] place and on those who live[d] there" (v. 28).

The event was so tragic that Jeremiah the prophet composed lamentations for Josiah. But in spite of these laments, the people marched relentlessly toward destruction within twenty-three years of Josiah's death. In fact, not more than three years after his death, the Babylonians, whom Josiah seemed to favor, took the first Hebrew captives in 606 B.C. including the prophet Daniel and his three friends. In 597 B.C. Ezekiel was taken into exile. Finally the whole city fell and was burned down, including the temple, in 586 B.C.

For one major blunder, a leader's whole career ended. Yet grace did not dwell on this sin or attribute the whole matter entirely to his one sin. Instead it attributed most of the cause to his grandfather Manasseh. Furthermore, the account of Josiah's life graciously ends not by underscoring the king's final weakness and disobedience, but by recalling Josiah's "acts of devotion" or "his goodness" (2 Chron 35:26). God's commendation was, "Well done, good and faithful servant." Thus out of tragedy, God was still working his purposes. What seemed a horrible end for God's faithful servant-king was in fact a reward. He was spared the horror of viewing the demise of everything the nation and God had built in Judah during the preceding millennium and a half.

· CHAPTER 37 ·

Let Us Send Away All These Women and Their Children

Then Shecaniah son of Jehiel . . . said to Ezra, "We have been unfaithful to our God by marrying foreign women from the peoples around us. But in spite of this, there is still hope for Israel. Now let us make a covenant before our God to send away all these women and their children, in accordance with the counsel of my lord and of those who fear the commands of our God. Let it be done according to the Law."

EZRA 10:2-3

The issue of divorce is never a pleasant topic, for those who are affected by it or for those who must interpret what the Scriptures say about it. A question of divorce makes our text a hard saying: Is divorce a morally proper corrective for apostasy? If so, how can this be squared with the outright statement in Malachi 2:16 that God hates divorce?

The marriage problems in Ezra 9—10 began in this way. In the seventh year of Artaxerxes (458 B.C.), Ezra led a second group of Jewish exiles from Babylon to Jerusalem, only to learn that a serious problem existed in the community that had developed previously under Zerubbabel. Influenced by leaders of the new

community in Jerusalem, the priests and Levites along with others in the city had intermarried with the pagan population they
had found living in the land. When Ezra learned this, he ripped
his garments and pulled out his hair in horror and grief. He was
dumbfounded as to what to do.

At the evening sacrifice, Ezra fell on his knees in prayer before
God, confessing his shame and guilt on behalf of his nation. As
he prayed, others joined him in weeping and prayer. Suddenly,
Shecaniah, one of the sons of Elam, proposed a solution: the
people would acknowledge their sin and make a covenant with
God that all pagan wives be put away. Ezra apparently agreed
that this was the mind of the Lord, and so an announcement was
made that in three days the putting away would take place.

On that third day, the people stood in the rain as Ezra intoned
these words, "You have been unfaithful; you have married foreign women, adding to Israel's guilt. Now make confession to the
LORD, the God of your fathers, and do his will. Separate yourselves from the peoples around you and from your foreign
wives" (Ezra 10:10-11).

Now according to the list in Ezra 10, only 113 had taken foreign wives (17 priests, 6 Levites, 1 singer, 3 porters and 86 laity).
Since the total number of families was something like 29,000, the
size of the problem shrinks under closer scrutiny to less than 4
men out of a 1000, or about 0.4 per cent. Nevertheless, the issue
was not size but the severing of Israel's marriage covenant with
God which forbade God's people marrying persons outside the
covenant.

Even before Israel had entered into the land, they had been
warned not to intermarry with the inhabitants (Ex 34:11-16;
Deut 7:1-5). Such intermarriage would inevitably result in idolatry. Though there were many intermarriages throughout Israel's history, apparently many of these involved proselytes. The
outstanding examples, of course, are Ruth, Rahab and Moses'

Cushite wife. But many others cannot be explained as converts; they often appear to be tolerated and left in the midst of God's people. Ultimately, this was one of the factors that led to God's judgment and the Babylonian captivity.

What did Ezra do with these wives? The word translated *to send away* or *to cause to go out* in Ezra 10:3 is not the usual word for *divorce*. Nevertheless, that is what appears to have happened. Even more surprising, their solution is said to agree with the law!

Divorce was permitted under certain circumstances in Deuteronomy 24:1-4. Could it be that Ezra unlocked the meaning of that mysterious phrase *for something unseemly, shameful* or as the New International Version translates *he finds something indecent about her?* This could not refer to adultery, as the law provided the death penalty in that case (Deut 22:28). Thus it had to be something else that brought shame on God's people. What could bring greater shame than the breaking of the covenant relationship and the ultimate judgment of God on all the people? I believe then that Ezra had this passage in mind when he observed the law and provided for the divorce of these unbelieving wives.

There are many questions that remain. Were the ostracized children and wives provided for? Were any attempts made to win them to faith in the one true God? No direct answers are given to these and similar questions, perhaps because these matters were not germane to the main point of revelation.

Those attempting to show that Ezra rendered a questionable decision when he took this tack point out that he lost his prestige and influence in the community as a result of this decision. However, when the chronology of Ezra and Nehemiah is restored to its proper sequence, according to the textual claims and the most recent studies from history, Ezra was once again before the public during the revival of Nehemiah in Nehemiah 8.

Are we left then with an argument for divorcing unbelieving spouses today? No! In fact, 1 Corinthians 7:12-16 says that if the unbeliever is willing to continue living with the believer, then they must not divorce, for the unbelieving partner is sanctified by the believer! However, should the unbeliever finally and irremediably desert the believer, the believer "is not bound in such circumstances; God has called us to live in peace" (1 Cor 7:15). The object is to win the unbelieving spouse to Christ. But when an unbeliever chooses to desert his or her partner and marriage vows, then reluctantly the believer may let that one go, that is, sadly accept the divorce with the right to be married to another. (See the discussion on Malachi 2:16 as well.)

· CHAPTER 38 ·

The King's Edict Granted the Jews the Right to Destroy

The king's edict granted the Jews in every city the right to assemble and protect themselves; to destroy, kill and annihilate any armed force of any nationality or province that might attack them and their women and children; and to plunder the property of their enemies.
ESTHER 8:11

Some object to this part of the Esther story, stating that no ruler would issue such an arbitrary decree sanctioning the slaughter of vast numbers of his subjects, including many unoffending citizens. But surely, the appeal is not based on history; these objectors have not read much about the extent or excesses of despotic power.

The real point is not the apparent injustice the Jews called for. Rather, it was the enormous unfairness of the king's original agreement with Haman to annihilate a total race of people. Therefore, if blame must be laid at someone's feet, it must be at King Xerxes' feet.

Some have attempted to build a case for the fact that Haman

was a descendant of the Amalekites whom Saul had been instructed to annihilate under the divine decree of the "ban" (see chapter 27). No certain evidence exists to certify this connection, however.

Whatever his motivation, Haman weaseled out of the king this foolish decree: "Dispatches were sent by couriers to all the king's provinces with the order to destroy, kill and annihilate all the Jews—young and old, women and little children—on a single day, the thirteenth day of the twelfth month, the month of Adar, and to plunder their goods" (Esther 3:13). Apparently, according to the laws of the Medes and the Persians, once a royal decree had been signed and issued it could not be retracted.

The only recourse that Xerxes had left was to countermand his previous decree with one extending the same privilege to the Jews. In fact, most have noted that Esther 8:11 is almost an exact duplicate of the original decree in Esther 3:13.

The posture of the Jews was one of self-defense. Their enemies attacked them with a vengeance, as can be seen in the death of 500 in the citadel of Susa alone. While this is not an incredibly large number, if the day's population of Susa was estimated at about half a million, it surely speaks of the danger the Jews faced as a result of the hatred Haman had fanned into existence. Had self-defense been denied the Jews, they would have been in deep trouble indeed.

The text consistently shows the Jews as morally superior to their oppressors. It records three times that the Jews did not take advantage of the royal provision to plunder (Esther 9:10, 15-16). Presumably, they also were allowed to put to death women and little children as well as the armed forces that came against them (3:13). This the Jews refused to do, in accordance with God's law. Instead, the text expressly says that they only put to death men (9:6, 12, 15). As defenders, the Jews did not attack nonmilitary targets. They themselves were the subjects of the attack.

In all the provinces, with an estimated population of one hundred million, seventy-five thousand of the enemy were slain. No mention is made of even one Jew being killed. (The Greek version of this same text puts the number at fifteen thousand slain.)

If some object that Esther was bloodthirsty in asking the king for a second day of such atrocities and killings (9:13), the response is found in 9:12 where Xerxes himself was concerned that the Jews needed to do more to protect themselves from oppression.

True, Esther is made of stern stuff, but her character is not one easily described as vindictive. Her request was only for an added day of self-defense, not additional days to carry the battle to their enemy's doorstep.

CHAPTER 39

Though God Slay Me, Yet Will I Hope in Him

*Though he slay me, yet will I hope
in him; I will surely defend my
ways to his face.*
JOB 13:15

The King James rendering of this verse is one of the most famous lines from the Old Testament: "Though he slay me, yet will I trust in him." However, this beautiful affirmation of trust, though retained by the New International Version has largely been abandoned by modern translators. Accordingly, the Revised Standard Version has, "Behold, he will slay me; I have no hope." This turns Job's determination to defend himself into what one writer called "a futile gesture of defiance, which he knows will be fatal."

This response by Job comes at the end of the first round of speeches and sets the scene for Job's second round with Eliphaz, Bildad and Zophar. Our hard saying comes in the midst of a speech (Job 12—14) exceeded in length only by Job's final speech in Job 29—31. The verses surrounding the text exude trust that Job will be vindicated (Job 13:18). He is prepared to defend himself and his ways, if need be, to God's face (13:15). His principle is stated in verse 16, "No godless man would dare come before him!" But that is just what Job claims he is not, "a godless man."

With Job's protests ringing in our ears, we may now attempt to understand verse 15. Job is not saying, as many moderns claim, that at the risk of a death he hopes Job is going to stand up for his rights and have his say—even if it kills him! This view assumes Job cares less about life than about ending his suffering and having his prosperity back.

But the view violates the flow of the context which we have just examined. Job does expect, at least at this point, to be vindicated. The pessimism of moderns and the Revised Standard Version just does not fit.

The chief translation problem is the verb, which can be translated *trust, wait, hesitate* or *tremble*. But the mood of the context should help us decide which it is. Whether Job's confidence is expressed as one of *waiting, hoping* or *trusting* is not half as important as the fact that he is confident and expects full vindication.

How then shall we translate the apparently negative statement in the Revised Standard Version's "I have no hope"? It is probably best handled as an assertative *la'*, which would be *certainly*, in place of the usual emphatic Hebrew *l*. We conclude that the Authorized Version's rendering is the one to retain. To agree with the Revised Standard Version would have Job staging a type of bravado which would end up being exactly what Job's wife advised him to do long before: "Curse God and die."

What does Job mean by the expression *Though he slay me?* It figuratively means "no matter what happens to me, I still remain confident that I will be vindicated, for I know I am innocent and I know the character of God."

·CHAPTER 40·

In My Flesh
I Will
See God

*Oh, that my words were recorded, that they were
written on a scroll, that they were inscribed with
an iron tool on lead, or engraved in rock forever!
I know that my Redeemer lives, and that in the end he
will stand upon the earth. And after my skin has been
destroyed, yet in my flesh I will see God; I myself
will see him with my own eyes—I, and not another.
How my heart yearns within me!*
JOB 19:23-27

Here is a passage notoriously difficult to translate yet celebrated
worldwide for the strong affirmation of faith in a bodily resurrection. Much depends on the authenticity and meaning of the
central declaration, "my Redeemer lives."

One point on which everyone can agree is that Job expected
to "see God," for he made the point three times in verses 26-27.
Nor did Job expect this visual experience to occur to a disembod-
ied shade or ghost. His references to the skin, flesh and the eyes
made that abundantly plain. He even used the emphatic pronoun

I three times in verse 27. It is clear: he expected personally to see God. But when?

Job was willing to stake his reputation on a future vindication of a permanent written record of his claims that he was innocent. Job wanted that record chiseled onto the hardest rock and then filled in with lead to lessen the chance that time or defacers would blot out the text.

One thing was sure, Job "knew that his Redeemer lives." The one who would stand up to defend Job was called his *Go'el*, his *kinsman redeemer* or *vindicator*. This kinsman-redeemer basically functioned as the avenger of the blood of someone unjustly fallen (2 Sam 14:11). He had the right to preempt all others in redeeming property left by a kinsman (Ruth 4:4-6). He also recovered stolen items (Num 5:8) or vindicated the rights of the oppressed (Prov 23:10-11). Therefore, he was one who redeemed, delivered and liberated.

In the Psalms, God was cast into this role of kinsman-redeemer (see Ps 19:14). God was that vindicator or redeemer for Job as well.

But when did Job hope to be cleared by God—before or after death? Apparently, as Job debated with his friends, he progressively lost hope in being cleared in this life (Job 17:1, 11-16). No, Job decided it would have to come after his death. But it would come. Hence the need for a written testimony of his complaint. Job believed that even if a person were cut down in life just as a tree was, the tree and the person would share the same hope— that a "shoot" would sprout out of the stump (Job 14:14). Even though it might take time (see *after* in Job 19:25-26), he hoped in the end for God's vindication.

In what state would Job be when that took place? Would he have a body or have only a spirit or even merely be a memory? Job believed he would have a body, for only from inside that body (v. 26) and with his own eyes (v. 27) would Job see God. He made the point that the experience would have a direct impact on his own eyeballs, and not on someone else's eyes. Thus Job was expecting a resurrection of his body! It was this which lay at the heart of his hope in God and in his vindication.

If some complain, as they surely will, that this is too advanced a doctrine for such primitive times as these (probably patriarchal times), I would respond that long before this, Enoch had been bodily translated into heaven (Gen 5:24). The fact that this mortal body could inhabit immortal realms should have settled the abstract question forever. Indeed, the whole economy of Egypt was tied to the expectation that bodily resurrection was not only possible but also probable. That expectation had functioned a full millennium and a half before Abraham went down into Egypt. Thus our modern complaints about bodily resurrections being advanced say more about modern problems than about ancient culture.

Job believed that he would be vindicated sooner or later, for his vindicator was able to do so, and he believed he would. Job gives much ground to the hope of a bodily resurrection even though this hope is found deep in the Old Testament.

· CHAPTER 41 ·

Man
Is But
a Maggot

*How then can a man be righteous before God? How
can one born of woman be pure? If even the
moon is not bright and the stars are not pure in
his eyes, how much less man, who is but a maggot
—a son of man, who is only a worm!*
JOB 25:4-6

T he speaker of this saying was Bildad, not the inspired writer Job.
However, Bildad was not all that original, especially in this final
round of speeches by Job's three "friends." Many of Bildad's best
lines were pirated either from Job or Eliphaz.

The first issue here is whether anything in this speech expresses God's point of view. Is it revelation or only an accurate
description of what took place, of no normative or prescriptive
value? Second, one must ask if Bildad's extreme position runs
counter to the truth that humans are made in God's image.

To the first question, most answer that what is recorded is
only descriptively true of what Bildad said, but not normative for
revelation. This is acceptable until what Bildad says involves con-

cepts that Job or God reinforce in the book itself. Then we may
be sure that those concepts too are normative for believers.

Bildad contrasted the imperfection of humanity with the majesty of God. In order to make his point, he modified the arguments of Eliphaz in Job 4:17-19 and 15:14-16. Indeed, the clause
How can a mortal be righteous before God? (25:4) reproduced verbatim
Job's question in Job 9:2. The second part of the line in verse 4
again borrowed from Job in Job 15:14: "What is man, that he can
be pure, or one born of woman, that he could be righteous?"
Thus the question was an authoritative one placing the allusion
to humans as being compared to maggots or worms in its proper
perspective.

This text must not be used to devalue the dignity or worth
that God has placed in men and women. They truly are made in
God's image. But nothing can better portray the relative position
of mortals when compared to God's majesty than these references to individuals as grubs or crawling earthworms. The statement is not an absolute one but one of comparison. Nothing
more vividly demonstrates the misery of man than Bildad's statement. The psalmist shared this sentiment when he bemoaned on
behalf of the Suffering Servant, "But I am a worm and not a
man" (Ps 22:6).

In Bildad's thought, as in Job 4:19 and 15:16, the emphasis falls
on the fragility and the corruptibility of mortal beings. This is
further emphasized by Bildad's word choices for *humans* that
stress weakness and their link to the soil.

The contrast is more striking after the soaring thought that
God is on high, reigning above. The same sentiment is even
found in an ancient Mesopotamian wisdom text which also
wrestled with theodicy. It asked, "Was ever sinless mortal born?"

Job answered that question with divine authority, "No, especially when you place mortal man next to the brilliant majesty
and the purity of the living God!"

· C H A P T E R 4 2 ·

I Have
Never Seen the
Righteous Forsaken

*I was young and now I am old, yet I have never
seen the righteous forsaken or their children
begging bread. They are always generous and
lend freely; their children will be blessed.*

PSALM 37:25-26

One wonders where the psalmist has been all his life if he has never
seen the righteous forsaken or their children begging bread.
Surely David was not speaking in any absolute sense, for he must
have seen just the reverse of what he stated here. So how can
Scripture be truthful when it includes such patently false statements as this one? Truly, we have here a hard saying!

But such treatment misses the psalmist's point. He did not
question that the righteous may be temporarily forsaken, needy
and poor. Rather, he observed that nowhere can it be shown that
the righteous have experienced *continued* desertion and destitution.

David himself had plenty of opportunity to complain that God had forgotten him. For example, he had to beg rich Nabal for bread. Therefore, it is important to note that David carefully sets his statement in the context of life's long haul, for he had been young and now he was much older.

Thus, what looks like continued desertion to those taking a short view of life is actually only a passing phase. A full trust in God will prove the reverse when life has been viewed from his perspective.

This acrostic psalm was designed to meet the very temptation assailing anyone in such dire circumstances. It contrasts what ultimately endures with the transitory. However, this does not mean God has not also provided, in some measure, relief even in this present life. As our Lord would later teach, much in accordance with some sentiments expressed here, those who seek first the kingdom of God will have all other things given to them according to their needs.

In fact, our Lord taught us to ask for our daily bread. Thus what is a command is also a promise. He invites us to pray for that which he wishes to give to us.

God does not abandon his people; he cares for them and provides for them. For those who have lived long enough in this world to see that God does finally right wrongs and avenge gross injustice, the psalmist's declarations ring true even if the short term offers many temporary exceptions.

If we are sure that God's watch-care includes his concern for even the small sparrows, should we assume that he will allow his children to go unloved and uncared for in this present age? While some may experience a temporary sense of being forsaken, that cannot and will not be their *continued* experience.

If it be objected, as I have already conceded, that some wrongs and deprivations never appear to be righted in this life, two further points must be made. First, the truth expressed here is proverbial in form. Proverbs gather up the largest amount of experience that fits the case without pausing to speak to the exceptions or to nuance the general teaching with the fewer, but real, objections. Such is the very nature of proverbs and the way we must understand them. If we press contemporary or biblical proverbs into being exhaustive treatments of every topic they comment on, our teaching and practice will become simplistic and reductionistic.

Second, the psalmist deliberately mentions the second generation as being the recipients of God's blessing. Thus, while some Third World peoples struggle with poverty, famine and starvation, out of the ashes of such real sorrow and pain often comes a whole new opportunity for the children who survive. The point is this: in the long haul, God does not forsake his own whether they have little or much; their children will be blessed!

CHAPTER 43

Awake, O Lord! Why Do You Sleep?

Awake, O Lord! Why do you sleep?
Rouse yourself! Do not reject us forever.
Why do you hide your face
and forget our misery and oppression?
We are brought down to the dust;
our bodies cling to the ground.
Rise up and help us;
redeem us because of your unfailing love.
PSALM 44:23-26

How strange is this accusation that the Lord may be sleeping and needs to be aroused when Psalm 121:4 asserts just the opposite: "Indeed, he who watches over Israel will neither slumber nor sleep." It was Baal, not God, who slept, according to the Canaanite tablets from Ugarit, Lebanon, and the tacit acknowledgement of the same by his prophets on Mount Carmel in their contest with Elijah (1 Kings 18:27).

Psalm 44 represents the believing community's search for answers after suffering military defeats of national proportion. The problem raised was this: if the king and the people have been faithful to the covenant (44:18-22), then why was God unfaithful to his promise to deliver and defend?

The root problem echoes that of Job, namely, the problem of God. But there is no attempt here to give either a theological or practical solution. In fact, this psalm is one of the clearest examples of a search for some cause or reason for national disasters besides deserved punishment by God for sin and guilt.

The answer, according to this psalm, comes when the psalmist exclaims in exasperation, "Yet *for your sake* we face death all day long" (v. 22). The wrath they experienced on this occasion had little to do with their sin but more to do with the spiritual battle between their enemies and the Lord these men and women served.

Theirs was a faith that went beyond any available evidences or handy theologies. But in the mystery of God, similar to the book of Job, these Jewish believers continued to believe, to trust and to pray.

Accordingly, the psalm contrasts the glorious past (vv. 1-8) with some present disaster (vv. 9-16). God seemed not to have been with the army (v. 9) when they had gone out to battle. Israel's defeat had made them a reproach and the scorn of their enemies (vv. 13-14). All this had happened even though Israel had not forgotten God (vv. 17-18); nevertheless, God had crushed them with a humiliating defeat (v. 19).

In spite of all of this ignominy and shame, their prayer and hope still centered on the Lord (vv. 23-26). This prayer is phrased in military terms. The call for God to awake and to arouse himself does not refer to sleep but a military action similar to that in the Song of Deborah in Judges 5:12: "Wake up, wake up, Deborah! Wake up, wake up, break out in song! Arise, O Barak! Take captive your captives." The same battle chant was used time and time again when the Ark of the Covenant was raised at the head of the procession as Israel went forth into battle:

"Whenever the ark set out, Moses said, 'Rise up, O LORD! May your enemies be scattered; may your foes flee before you' " (Num 10:35). The prayer is for divine help in the crisis which may have continued even though the battle had been lost. Perhaps the same war continued. "Rise up and help us" (Ps 44:26), they cried in the psalm. But the final word of the psalm is the confidence that God would yet help them because of his *unfailing love*—that word of grace which occurs in the Old Testament over two hundred and fifty times and speaks of God's unmerited loving-kindness, mercy and grace (v. 26).

Therefore, this psalm does not contradict the psalm which assures us that our God never slumbers nor sleeps. He does not! That God sometimes defers his punishments and extends apparently unwarranted tolerance to the wicked and their evil indicates to the superficial observer that God sleeps and needs rousing. But such divine long-suffering and mercy must not be confused with indifference or unawareness on his part. Furthermore, the language is not, as we have already stated, the language of weariness or slumber, but the language of a call for God to march forth in militant arms to defend his holy name and his kingdom.

CHAPTER 44

Man Is Like the Beasts That Perish

But man, despite his riches, does not endure;
he is like the beasts that perish. . . .
A man who has riches without understanding
is like the beasts that perish.
PSALM 49:12, 20

This twice repeated refrain (with similar, but not identical, words), not only divides the psalm into two major parts (introduction—vv. 1-4; first section—vv. 5-12; second section—vv. 13-20), but also introduces what appears to be an unexpectedly pessimistic statement comparing human death to that of the beasts! Thus the "riddle" (v. 4) that the psalm introduces is not the Samson type of riddle, but the riddle of life itself. What is the relationship of life to death? And is human life (and death) different in any significant way from that of animals?

Apparently, the psalmist was in the midst of some grave situation. In such times of despair, it was and still is all too easy to compare one's own desperate situation with the wicked's luxurious successes. These proud despisers of religion boasted of their riches and flaunted their wealth in the faces of the godly.

But did such success also insure, as these arrogant sinners seemed to infer, that their wealth and privilege would carry over into the world after death? It was on that point that the psalmist began to get some perspective for the fears haunting him. Indeed, a person's wealth could not redeem his or her person, family or goods; mortals could not pay their own ransoms (vv. 7-8). When the wealthy sinner died, everything was left behind.

Therefore, in that sense death was the great leveler of all life, whether it was animal or human life. For everyone, the grave was the prospect, unless something else intervened. If money had been the criterion for gaining eternal life, then the rich should have achieved everlasting life. But that is patently incorrect, for neither one's position or wealth has yet to buy an escape from the grim reaper, death.

It is against this background, and only on this comparative basis, that we are warned that "humankind does not survive" (v. 12), that is to say, *endure,* or literally *lodge overnight.* Hence the text is ironic, for in searching for permanency through position or wealth, the realities of life assured no such guarantee. Death would cut down all beings, human and animal, without respect to influence, wealth or power.

To trust in one's self or wealth, consequently, was highest folly. Old Testament wisdom literature expresses the opposite value of those who trust in themselves, namely, the fear of the Lord. Not only was the fear of the Lord the beginning of knowledge (Prov 1:7), it was also that which made possible the elimination of two possible fears found in this psalm: the fear of one's enemies in times of affliction (49:5) and the fear of the advantage of wealth in the face of death (vv. 16-19).

But verse 15 is the most reassuring truth in this psalm: "But

God will redeem my life [literally, *my soul*] from the grave; he will surely take me to himself." Few words could be more succinct and hopeful than these, yet so many scholars and readers prefer to be obtuse when attempting to understand this psalm.

In spite of the psalmist's somewhat embarrassing position in the areas of power, position or finances, he had a confidence which money could not purchase. He knew the grave would not seal his doom and end his hope of any more life; it could only be the place from which God would rescue him and redeem him. There is no doubt that the word *soul* in this passage functions, as it does in so many, as the expression for the personal pronoun *me*.

If all men, women and beasts are led like sheep to the grave so that death feeds on them (v. 14), doubtless a strong contrast has begun to set in already in the second half of verse 14. This contrast is completed in verse 15. God himself will step in and ransom those who fear him from the power of death and the grave.

There is more. God will "take," or "receive" those who so believe in him, "to himself." This word *to take* or *receive* is more positive than it might first sound. It is an allusion to God's "taking" Enoch to heaven in Genesis 5:24. Enoch no longer walked this earth when God suddenly came and took him to be with him. This clearly says that all believers will be resurrected and defeat death. This is a hope which exceeds any that even the rich and the mighty possess.

Psalm 73:24 expresses similar confidence: "You guide me with your counsel, and afterward you will take me into glory." The hope being held out here is the hope of the resurrection, just as it is offered in Psalm 49:15. Why, you ask, are the rich compared to the beasts if the text only contrasts the believer who fears God and the unbeliever who fears nothing since he or she has all the power money can buy?

In answer, those in positions of honor and wealth can be so brutish in their thinking and living that they may as well be animals. They are "without understanding" (v. 20). It is for this reason that the psalm calls for "all . . . peoples" to "listen" (v. 1) and to find "understanding" (v. 3) unless, of course, they wish to be like the beasts and brutes without understanding. In their death they too will be like the beasts: they will perish.

The lesson of the "riddle" is clear: Do not trust in yourself or your riches to save you or to give eternal life; only God can ransom you from the grave and take you to himself!

· C H A P T E R   4 5 ·

Great Was the Company of Those Who Proclaimed the Word

The Lord announced the word,
and great was the company of those who proclaimed it.
PSALM 68:11

Perhaps many will remember the great chorus from Handel's *Messiah* based on this psalm. The loud acclamation rings out: "The Lord gave the word! Great was the company of the preachers." What may not be so obvious is that this is a "hard saying" for those who believe all of Scripture restricts women from preaching. Two major issues have been associated with this text: (1) What was the word that was announced? and (2) Were the announcers women?

The first problem is the less difficult one. "The word" (*'omer*) in this context hardly means mere news, say, of the victory that had just been won. It is a divine word, either of promise (Ps 77:8) or command with accompanying divine power (Hab 3:9), or else it is his word which is likened elsewhere to a mighty thunder or a trumpet blast (Ps 68:33; Is 30:30; Zech 9:14).

The older commentators found in this *word* a reference to gospel preaching, probably because they linked this text directly with Isaiah 40:9. That meaning well fits the Isaiah context, but no direct reference to preaching the good news or gospel appears in this context.

It would be too reductionistic, however, to limit this word, as many unfortunately do, to a watchword in war. Now it is true that women were leaders of the songs of victory and the feminine gender is used for *announcers*. It will be remembered that when Israel defeated Pharaoh, Deborah and Barak overthrew Sisera, Jephthah routed the Ammonites and David beat Goliath, the women went forth with a song of victory.

But a song of victory from God does not appear to cover all that this psalm talks about. It is used of the word of promise as well, and this is what opens this text up for a larger sphere of reference. Therefore, everything included in that word of promise was being communicated to a great host who would announce that word.

As mentioned before, the announcers of the good news *(hamebasserim)* appear to be women, for the Hebrew participle is in the feminine plural form. God placed his word in the mouths of his announcers; the word of promise and power in the face of a hostile world. As such, this word is very close to that of Isaiah 40:9 and especially Joel 2:28-29. These heralders comprised a great host of individuals. Surely this foreshadows what God would do at Pentecost and what he has since done all over the world through the great missionary force which has included so many women. Those in search of Scripture passages restricting women from preaching will need to look elsewhere for support.

• C H A P T E R 4 6 •

God Presides among the "Gods"

God presides in the great assembly;
he gives judgment among the "gods."
PSALM 82:1

We are surprised to find a biblical text appearing to acknowledge the tacit existence of gods rivaling Yahweh. The singer Asaph beholds Elohim presiding over a great congregation and rendering judgments before what the text innocently refers to as "gods." Does this perhaps unexpurgated passage confirm polytheism?

Before us is a courtroom. The matter before the court is the ever-present, nettlesome problem of the wicked and the injustices which seem to sweep along in their path.

In addressing the "gods" (in Hebrew, *elohim*), God is not acknowledging pagan deities or recognizing the existence of other supernatural beings like himself; rather, he is addressing the earthly judges and administrators of his law whom he has set up to represent him. Our Lord depends on these administrators, functioning as magistrates in the divinely ordained state, to bring a measure of immediate relief from the injustices and brutalities of life.

This usage of the Hebrew word *elohim* is not as unusual as it might appear at first. Other passages refer to this class of Israelite rulers and judges as God's representatives on earth. Accordingly, Exodus 21:6, using the same word, orders the slave who voluntarily wishes to be indentured for life to be taken "before the judges." Likewise, Exodus 22:8 advises the owner who complains of a theft, even when no thief has been found, to "appear before the judges." Using the same word, the psalmist affirmed in Psalm 138:1, "I will praise you, O LORD, with all my heart; before the 'gods' [which would be better read *rulers* or *judges*] I will sing your praise."

Therefore, it should not be altogether surprising that Psalm 82:1 and 6 should use this same word to refer to the executive or judicial branches of government—or that scholars have translated the word as "gods" in the past. In fact, verse 6 of this chapter makes the case crystal clear by making all believers who "are sons of the Most High" to be "gods."

It was Psalm 82:6 that our Lord appealed to in John 10:34 by saying, when he was accused of blasphemy for claiming that he was God, "Is it not written in your Law, 'I have said you are "gods" '?" In so doing, Jesus was demonstrating that the title could be attached to certain men "to whom the word of God came" (Jn 10:35), and therefore there could not be any prima facie objections lodged against his claim to be divine. There was a legitimate attachment of the word *elohim* to those people who had been specially prepared by God to administer his law and word to the people.

Ever since Genesis 9:6, God had transferred to humankind the
execution of his personal prerogative of determining life and
death and had instituted among them an office which bore the
sword. God had transferred the exercise of his power to these
subordinate "gods" without thereby divesting himself of ultimate
say.

God now sits in judgment of these magistrates, for all they do
goes on before his eyes. The question from on high is, "How long
will you defend the unjust and show partiality to the wicked?"
This is the great assembly over which our Lord presides and the
ones he now questions for their shabby handling of the complaints of the oppressed. But there is no hint of a belief in many
gods or goddesses. Nor does God thereby imply they have the
divine nature exclusive to the Trinity. It is simply a case where
one term, *elohim*, must do double duty when it refers not only to
God, but to his special servants appointed for the unique tasks
described in these contexts.

· C H A P T E R 4 7 ·

God Turned Their Hearts to Hate His People

Then Israel entered Egypt;
Jacob lived as an alien in the land of Ham.
The LORD made his people very fruitful;
he made them too numerous for their foes,
whose hearts he turned to hate his people,
to conspire against his servants.
PSALM 105:23-25

Once again we encounter a passage which appears to make God the author of evil, in this case the Egyptian hostility toward the Hebrew slaves. Some have tried to soften the strength of the expression by converting the *he turned* into a passive form, *their hearts were turned*. However, the text does not warrant this. Similar difficulties arise in Exodus 9:12, Isaiah 6:9-10, Mark 4:12, John 12:39-40 and Romans 11:8. (See our discussion of Exodus 9:12 about God's hardening Pharaoh's heart.) The hard saying before us is another instance in which we will have to distinguish between the permissive will of God and his directive will concerning evil.

The third strophe (vv. 24-36) in Psalm 105 centers on the Lord's control of the events of history. Even acts of enmity, and the crafty schemes of a Pharaoh bent on destroying God's people, were under the control of Israel's Lord.

Just as Judas's act of treachery against our Lord was part of the "cup which the Father had given [Christ]," so Pharaoh's treachery against Israel was no less part of the plan and the overall superintendence of the living God.

Not that God is the immediate author of everything he permits or allows to bring glory to his name. It happened that the Old Testament writers did not feel the need to distinguish between primary and secondary causation. For them everything was ordained and designed by God. Even sin itself did not appear uncontrolled; it too was superintended by God. The guilt and the responsibility for sin rested, nevertheless, with those who had sinned.

Hence, in this sense God hardened Pharaoh's heart, put a lying spirit in the mouth of the false prophets, did evil to a city as well as good, and the like. Since these Old Testament worthies saw the finger of God even in life's smallest detail, and rested content in the certain knowledge that God was in charge of everything, we must not expect them to distinguish sharply between an action viewed as a *consequence* and the same action viewed as the *end* of another action.

Since God was ultimately in charge and was able to make even the wrath of a human praise his name, Pharaoh's hatred for God's people may be said to come from him. But in the sense that these acts were also sinful and deserving of punishment, the real agents of this hate and conspiracy were none other than Pharaoh and the Egyptians themselves.

CHAPTER 48

Happy Is He Who Dashes Your Infants against the Rocks

O Daughter of Babylon, doomed to destruction,
happy is he who repays you
for what you have done to us—
he who seizes your infants
and dashes them against the rocks.
PSALM 137:8-9

Many a tenderhearted believer has read these words with shock and chagrin. They are frankly at a loss to explain how one could speak with what appears to be such malice, vindictiveness and delight concerning the sufferings of others. How can the gentleness of the opening verses of this psalm be harmonized with the call for such brutal revenge in the last verses?

This psalm is just one of six psalms that are generally classified as *imprecatory* psalms. These are Psalms 55, 59, 69, 79, 109, and 137. There is no author or title to Psalm 137; however, the scene is pictured as taking place "by the rivers of Babylon." Psalm 79 is ascribed to Asaph; the remaining four are from David's pen, according to the ancient psalm titles. The label *imprecatory* may be misleading if it is not used to denote its more proper sense of invoking judgment, calamity or curse in an appeal to God who alone is the judge of all beings.

But how, you ask, can it ever be right to wish or pray for the destruction or doom of others as is done in at least portions of these psalms? Could a Christian ever indulge in such a prayer?

These invocations are not mere outbursts of a vengeful spirit; they are, instead, prayers addressed to God. These earnest pleadings to God ask that he step in and right some matters so grossly distorted that if his help does not come all hope for justice is lost.

These hard sayings are legitimate expressions of longings of Old Testament saints for the vindication that only God's righteousness can bring. They are not statements of personal vendetta, but they are utterances of zeal for the kingdom of God and his glory. To be sure, the attacks which provoked these prayers were not from personal enemies; rather, they were rightfully seen as attacks against God and especially his representatives in the promised line of the Messiah. Thus, David and his office bore the brunt of most of these attacks, and this was tantamount to an attack on God and his kingdom!

It is frightening to realize that a righteous person may, from time to time, be in the presence of evil and have little or no reaction to it. But in these psalms we have the reverse of that situation. These prayers were the fierce abhorrence of sin from those who wanted to see God's name and cause triumph. Therefore, those whom the saints oppose in these prayers were the fearful embodiments of wickedness.

Since David was by far the author of more imprecatory psalms than anyone else, let it also be noted that David exhibited just the opposite of a vindictive or revengeful spirit in his own life. He was personally assaulted time and time again by the likes of a Shimei, a Doeg, a cunning Saul, and his own son Absalom.

Never once did he attempt to effect his own vindication or lift his hand to exercise what many may have regarded as his prerogative as royalty.

In fact, even some of these very psalms where he and others pray for God speedily to vindicate his own honor and name, David, and the other psalmists who pray in a similar manner, protest that they have kind thoughts toward these same evildoers. Thus in Psalm 35:12-14, David mourns, "They repay me evil for good and leave my soul forlorn. Yet when they were ill, I put on sackcloth and humbled myself with fasting. When my prayers returned to me unanswered, I went about mourning as though for my friend or brother. I bowed my head in grief as though weeping for my mother."

Finally, these imprecations only repeat in prayer what God had already stated elsewhere would be the fate of those who were impenitent and who were persistently opposing God and his kingdom. In almost every instance, each expression used in one of these prayers of malediction may be found in plain prose statements of what will happen to those sinners who persist in opposing God. Compare, for example, such expressions in Psalm 37:2, 9-10, 15, 35-36, 38; 55:23; 63:9-11; and 64:7-9.

But let us apply these principles to the special problems of Psalm 137:8-9, which many regard as the most difficult of all the imprecatory psalms. First, the word *happy* is used altogether twenty-six times in the book of Psalms. It is used only of individuals who trust God. It is not an expression of a sadistic joy in the ruin or destruction of others.

The words *dashes [your infants] against the rocks* are usually regarded as being so contrary to the teachings of the New Testament that there is little need to discuss the matter any further. Curiously enough, these very same words are repeated in the New Testament by no one less than our Lord, in Luke 19:44. In fact, the verb in its Greek form is found only in Psalm 137:9 (in the Septuagint, the Greek translation of the Hebrew text) and in the lament of our Lord over Jerusalem in Luke 19:44. This is the clearest proof possible that our Lord was intentionally referring to this psalm. Moreover, our Lord found no more difficulty in quoting this psalm than he did in quoting the other two psalms most filled with prayers of imprecation, namely, Psalm 69 and 109.

God "shattered the enemy" at the Red Sea (Ex 15:6) and he will continue to do so through the triumph of his Son as he "will rule them with a rod of iron" and "dashes them to pieces like pottery" (Rev 2:26-27; 12:5; 19:15).

The word translated *infant* is somewhat misleading. The Hebrew word does not specify age, for it may mean a very young or a grown child. The word focuses on a relationship and not on age; as such, it points to the fact that the sins of the fathers were being repeated in the next generation.

That the psalmist has located the site of God's judgment in Babylon not only appears to denote this psalm as being composed while Judah was in exile in Babylon but also that there are figurative elements included in the psalm. One thing Babylon was devoid of was rocks or rocky cliffs against which anything could be dashed. In fact there were not any stones available for building, contrary to the rocky terrain of most of Palestine. All building had to depend on the production of sun-dried mud bricks and the use of bituminous pitch for mortar. Therefore when the psalmist speaks of "dashing [infants] against the rocks," he is speaking figuratively and metaphorically. Close to this metaphorical use of the same phrase is that of Psalm 141:6, "Their rulers will be thrown down from the cliffs." But that same psalm adds, "And the wicked will learn that my words were well spoken [the literal rendering is *sweet*]." If the rulers had literally been tossed over a cliff, they surely would have had a hard time hearing anything!

What, then, does "Happy is he who repays you for what you have done to us—he who seizes your infants and dashes them against the rocks" mean? It means that God will destroy Babylon and her progeny for her proud assault against God and his kingdom. But those who trust in God will be blessed and happy. For those who groaned under the terrifying hand of their captors in Babylon there was the prospect of a sweet, divine victory that they would share in as sons and daughters of the living God. As such, this is a prayer which Christians may also pray, so long as it is realized that what is at stake is not our own reputation or our personal enemies, but the cause of our Lord's great name and kingdom.

The point remains: these psalms of cursing do not contain "wicked" or "immoral" requests or desires. They only plead with God that he not let the office of the Messiah or the Messiah's kingdom be trampled underfoot by the arrogant despisers of those who currently hold that office and throne.

• C H A P T E R 4 9 •

A Bribe Concealed Pacifies Great Wrath

*A gift given in secret soothes anger,
and a bribe concealed in the cloak pacifies great wrath.*
PROVERBS 21:14

At first blush, this proverb appears to commend bribery. It reads as
if bribery is God's approved way of dealing with certain, or even
most, adverse circumstances. But this first reading cannot be
sustained, for the proverb does not commend bribery but, rather,
good sense. The point is this: when someone is angry with you,
sue for peace as quickly as possible. At that time, genuine peace
is more important than how it is cloaked or the form it comes.
Pacifying the angry person is often one's first duty, and the price
of peace is much smaller than the cost of anger and constant
strife.

This is borne out in everyday life. Often, logical arguments are
not half as effective in winning the day as some token of esteem

or appreciation. Consider the person who has quarreled with his or her spouse and decides to give up arguing about who was right and who was wrong in favor of offering a gift of appreciation. At times this strategy wins the peace and effects more harmony than acting like a collegiate debater.

In the same light, Jesus, in the Sermon on the Mount, encouraged his followers to give a cloak or an additional mile of service when coerced to give the first. Certainly, such acts could well be interpreted as offering a gift to assuage the wrath of those with jurisdiction over them. This kind of gift is not what we would call a bribe. It is a gift given in good conscience to achieve a righteous end.

Of course we are dealing with a proverb. Therefore, this statement must not be absolutized, for if it were, it could be made to teach the false conclusion that we must sue for peace at any price and under any conditions. The book of Proverbs, instead, picks up the largest number of cases and puts its teaching in the broadest perspective possible. However, we would be scandalized to hear a pastor from an American pulpit urging believers to bribe state officials under certain circumstances.

How, then, can we resolve this apparent conflict of interests? Some suggest that the Bible only condemns the taking of bribes, since it is assumed that the godly person will carry out God's law without needing to be prodded by payoffs. This argument would disallow accepting bribes for one's own personal profit, especially for perverting justice or administering justice that the public already deserves. With that part of the argument we can agree.

But some may further claim that the Bible nowhere condemns giving bribes to impede the progress of apostate governments. Here we must proceed with caution. If this type of bribery is grouped with treason or spying under certain conditions of war or enemy occupation of one's native land, it should be treated separately from a general statement on bribery.

The most basic teaching of bribe-taking is found in Exodus 23:8, "Do not accept a bribe, for a bribe blinds those who see and twists the words of the righteous." That same warning is repeated for rulers in Deuteronomy 16:18-19, "Appoint judges and officials . . . [who] do not pervert justice or show partiality [or who] do not accept a bribe, for a bribe blinds the eyes of the wise and twists the words of the righteous." The point is clear: bribery perverts the justice for the sake of personal gain.

Solomon made the same point in Proverbs 17:8, "A bribe is a charm to the one who gives it; wherever he turns, he succeeds." Again in Proverbs 17:23 it warns, "A wicked man accepts a bribe in secret to pervert the course of justice."

This perversion is well illustrated in the lives of Samuel's sons in 1 Samuel 8:3: "But his sons did not walk in his ways. They turned aside after dishonest gain and accepted bribes and perverted justice." And that was the sin mentioned by Isaiah (Is 1:23), Amos (Amos 5:12) and the psalmist (Ps 26:10). The evil side of bribery lies in the perversion of justice—taking gifts for personal gain when justice and leadership should be granted without them. When Jehoshaphat warned the newly appointed judges to "judge carefully, for with the LORD our God there is no injustice or partiality or bribery ['taking of gifts']" (2 Chron 19:7), he was not excluding all gift giving, as 2 Chronicles 32:23 shows. He was condemning gifts meant to pervert judgment.

Thus gifts, like all gain from this world, can carry with them great danger when they threaten to rearrange a person's general scale of values and purposes for doing things. But they are highly acceptable when they are used in a responsible way and given without any implied or explicit demand for a favor in return. They even are commended when used to cool down the wrath of an enemy, a foe or a relative who may be temporarily out of control. These gifts could avoid great wrath, yet they would also be called a bribe in Scripture.

• CHAPTER 50 •

Train a Child in the Way He Should Go

Train a child in the way he should go,
and when he is old he will not turn from it.
PROVERBS 22:6

What makes this text a hard saying is not the meaning of the words as they stand; they are plain and easy to translate. Instead, the problem centers in the differing views of the central phrase, *the way he should go,* and with the fact that the verse doesn't always "come true."

Readers often assume this verse is a promise without any exception given to all godly parents: Raise your children as moral, God-fearing believers, and God promises that they will turn out all right in the end. But what about children raised in just such a Christian home who appear to abandon their faith or lapse into immorality?

To answer this extremely important question, which has been debated with such vigor and passion, it is best to start with an analysis of the text itself. *Train a child in the way he should go* means to dedicate something or someone for the service of God. The verb is found in Deuteronomy 20:5 and in the parallel passages on the temple dedication in 1 Kings 8:63 and 2 Chronicles 7:5. In its noun form it is the name of the Jewish feast of Hanukkah.

The resulting range of meanings for this act of dedication includes: to prepare a child for service, to dedicate a child to God or to train a child for adulthood. Parents are urged to dedicate and begin training each child as an act of dedication to the living God.

But interpretation problems emerge as soon as we look for an antecedent for the pronoun in the phrase *according to his way*, translated above as *in the way he should go*. Literally, the phrase is *according to the mouth of,* which has led some to suggest *in accordance with the training he received at his "beginning."* However, the use of the word *mouth* for this concept instead of the word *beginning* would be strange indeed. Or it could be rendered more generally, *after the measure of, conformably to* or *according to his way.*

What is the "way?" It could mean the way that the child ought to go according to God's law: the proper way in light of God's revelation. It could also mean the way best fitting the child's own personality and particular traits.

Which is correct? There is no doubt that the first presents the highest standard and more traditional meaning. However, it has the least support from the Hebrew idiom and seems to be a cryptic way to state what other proverbial expressions would have done much more explicitly.

Therefore, we conclude that this enigmatic phrase means that instruction ought to be conformed to the nature of the youth. It ought to regulate itself according to the stage of life, evidence of God's unique calling of the child and the manner of life for which God is singling out that child. This does not give the child a carte blanche to pick and choose what he or she wishes to learn. It does, however, recognize that the training children receive must often be as diverse and unique as the number of children God has given to us.

The result will be, as the second line of the proverb underscores, that *even* "when he gets old he will not turn from it." The *from it* refers to the training of youth which was conformed to God's work in the child's very nature and being. This training became so imbued, inbred and accustomed that it was almost second nature.

As with many other moral proverbs of this sort, the question often comes from many a distraught parent: "Does this proverb have any exceptions to it, or will it always work out that if we train our children as this verse advises us, we can be sure they won't turn from the Lord?"

No, this verse is no more an ironclad guarantee than is any other proverb in this same literary category. As in many other universal or indefinite moral prescriptions (proverbs), it tells us only what generally takes place without implying there are no exceptions to the rule. The statement is called a proverb, not a promise. Many godly parents have raised their children in ways that were genuinely considerate of the children's own individuality and the high calling of God, yet the children have become rebellious and wicked despite their parents' attempts to bring about different results.

There is, however, the general principle which sets the standard for the majority. This principle urges parents to give special and detailed care as to the awesome task of rearing children so that the children may continue in that path long after the lessons have ceased.

CHAPTER 51

Where There Is No Vision the People Perish

Where there is no revelation, the people cast off all restraint; but blessed is he who keeps the law.
PROVERBS 29:18

For many years this proverb has been misinterpreted, probably because the King James Version translates it: "Where there is no vision, the people perish." One can infer from that translation that wise groups must have a five-, ten- or twenty-year plan for the future if they do not wish to become defunct as an organization. And many have taken just that meaning from this text.

However, the word *vision* does not refer to one's ability to formulate future goals and plans. Instead, it is a synonym for the prophetic word itself. It is what a prophet does. It refers to the prophetic vision, revelation which comes as the word of God.

Israel endured times when the prophetic word was silent.

When Samuel was a young boy, "in those days the word of the LORD was rare" (1 Sam 3:1). For all the times Israel rejected the word, God sent a famine on the earth; not a famine, mind you, of food and water, but an even more damaging famine: a famine of the word of God (Amos 8:12; see also 2 Chron 15:3; Ps 74:9).

Besides *vision*, a second key word has been misunderstood in this verse: the word *perish*. This does not refer to the perishing of churches with inactive planning committees (a fact which may be true on grounds other than those presented here in this text). Nor does it mean the perishing of the unevangelized heathen who will die in their sin if someone does not reach them quickly (a fact which is also true on other grounds).

The word translated in the King James Version as "perish" has a very impressive background to it. It means "to cast off all restraint." It clearly warns that where the word of God is silenced so that it no longer comments on the local situation, the results are terrifying. The populace becomes ungovernable as they cast aside all that is decent and civil for that which their own baser appetites wish to indulge in.

The best picture of how this takes place can be found in Exodus 32:25. While Moses was absent for a mere forty days on Mt. Sinai receiving the Law of God, the people began to fear that he would never return. Without the input of the prophetic word, the people began to get out of control. They cast off all restraint and began to dance about a newly formed golden calf. They ate and drank and indulged in open immorality, apparently recalling what they had seen in Egypt.

Without the announcement of the word of God, teaches this text, the people will become unrestrained, disorderly and grossly obscene in their manner of life. The verb means to "let loose," that is "to let one's hair down," whether literally or figuratively (see also Lev 13:45; Num 5:18; and perhaps Judg 5:2).

On the other hand, continues our proverb, "Blessed is he who keeps the law." Thus, on the one hand, a people is in an untenable position when the voice of the preacher ceases, because they let loose and nothing is left to restrain them; but, on the other hand, they are only truly happy when they have the good fortune of possessing the word of God and then place themselves under the hearing and doing of that word.

CHAPTER 52

There Is Nothing Better Than to Eat, Drink and Find Satisfaction

A man can do nothing better than to eat and drink and find
satisfaction in his work. This too, I see, is from the hand of
God, for without him, who can eat or find enjoyment? To the
man who pleases him, God gives wisdom, knowledge and happiness,
but to the sinner he gives the task of gathering and
storing up wealth to hand it over to the one who
pleases God. This too is meaningless, a chasing after the wind.
ECCLESIASTES 2:24-26

All too often the writer of Ecclesiastes has been blamed for all too much. For example, in the text before us, it is not uncommon to hear shouts charging the writer with epicureanism, that is, the philosophy which advises us to eat, drink and be merry for we only go around once and then we die!

But this charge is false on several counts. For one thing, the text has not been translated correctly. For another, it misses the point that death is not the natural sequel to eating and drinking. Instead, the text insists that even such mundane experiences as eating and drinking are gifts from the hand of a gracious God.

But let us begin with the translation issue. Literally rendered, the text here affirms, "There is not a good [inherent?] in a person that he [or she] should be able to eat, drink or get satisfaction from his [or her] work. Even this, I realized, was from the hand [or "the power"] of God." This translation avoids the phrase *there is nothing better*. Even though such a comparative form does exist in a somewhat similar formula in Ecclesiastes 3:12 and 8:15, it does not appear in this context.

Scholars uniformly assume that the word for *better* has dropped out of this context, but there is no evidence to back up that assumption. Furthermore, the writer is not saying at this point that no other options exist for the race other than to try calmly to enjoy the present. This indeed would be a hedonistic and materialistic philosophy of life which would effectively cut God off from any kind of consideration.

The Preacher's point is not one of despair—"There's nothing left for us to do than the basically physical acts of feeding one's face and trying to get as many kicks out of life as we can." Rather, his point is that whatever good or value is to be found, its worth cannot be determined merely by being part of the human race.

We mortals must realize that if we are to achieve satisfaction and pleasure from anything in life, even things as base and mundane as eating and drinking, we must realize that all of this comes from the hand of God. The source of pleasure, joy and goodness does not reside in the human person as humanism or idealism would want us to believe.

Verse 25 is more adamant on this point. Who will be able to find any enjoyment unless they first find the living God who is the only true source of all joy, satisfaction and pleasure? The text assures us that "without him," such satisfaction is a lost search.

The ground for the distribution of this joy is carefully set forth in verse 26: it is a matter of pleasing God first. The opposite of

pleasing God is "one who continues to live in sin." This same
contrast between pleasing God and being a sinner is found in
Ecclesiastes 7:26 and 8:12-13. Or, another way to define the
one continually choosing sin is "one who does not fear God."

Such a call to please God as a basis for realizing joy, pleasure
and satisfaction, is not, as some claim, too cheery a note for
such a pessimistic book. The truth of the matter is that all too
many have missed the positive note that is deeply rooted in the
repeated refrains in Ecclesiastes.

God will grant three gifts to those who please him: wisdom,
knowledge and joy. But to the sinner who persists in trying to
remake God's world, there is also an outcome: "a chasing after
the wind." This reference to the chasing of wind is to the frus-
trating activity in which the sinner works night and day to heap
things up only to find in the end that he must, and as a matter
of fact does, turn them over to the one who pleases God.

If only the sinner would come to know God and please him,
then he too would receive the ability to find joy in all of life just
as the one who fears God has found.

· CHAPTER 53 ·

Man's Fate Is
Like That
of the Animals

*Man's fate is like that of the animals; the same fate
awaits them both: As one dies, so dies the other. All have
the same breath; man has no advantage over the animal.
Everything is meaningless. All go to the same place; all
come from dust, and to the dust all return. Who knows
if the spirit of man rises upward and if the spirit of the
animal goes down into the earth?*
ECCLESIASTES 3:19-21

If ever there were a hard saying in the Scriptures, this would surely be among the most difficult! It is bad enough that death seems to unfairly level all humans—young or old, good or bad. But this saying casts a grim shadow that appears to say that all hope is lost after death as well—a startling statement indeed! Is it true that men and beasts have about the same hope for any kind of life after death? Is it really only a matter of "fate"? These are some of the questions this text raises.

First, the word *fate* is an overtranslation. The word that appears here is merely the word *happening*. Thus, no references are made to chance, luck or ill fortune. It is solely the fact that one happening, one event—namely, death—overtakes all things that share mortality.

The text then affirms that "all go to the same place." But the place that is intended here is not oblivion or nonexistence; it is rather the grave! Certainly, both men and beasts are made out of dust and therefore it is to the dust that they will return. In that sense, as one dies, so dies the other. Death is no respecter of persons or animals!

But most disturbing about those who insist on this hopeless view of death in the Old Testament is the way they translate some texts in order to substantiate their own views. In the clearest tones possible in the Hebrew, verse 21 states that "the spirit of man goes upward, but the spirit of the beast goes down to the earth." The verbs *to go upward* and *to go downward* are active participles with the sign of the article. There is no need to say that Hebrew has confused the article with a slightly different reading for the interrogative.

Furthermore, had not Solomon already argued in this very context that the unjust judges would face the living God at the last judgment (3:17)? How could they do this if it was all over when they died? And did not Solomon warn just as forcibly that the final judgment of God would bring every earthly deed into the light of his justice (12:7, 14)? But if it were the end of existence, who would care about such idle threats that warned about a later judgment?

The concept that people could and did live after death is as old as Enoch himself. That man, it is recorded in Genesis 5:24, entered into the eternal state with his body! Likewise, the patriarch Job knew that a person would live again if he died, just as a tree sometimes would sprout shoots after it too had been cut down (Job 14:7, 14).

Nor should we stress too much the statement *Who knows,* as

if the text gives us a question for which there is no answer. In the nine places where this expression occurs in Scripture, only three are actually questions (Esther 4:14; Eccles 2:19; 6:12). In the two passages that are similar to our text, it is followed by a direct object. The statement is a rhetorical remark that calls for us to remember that it is God who knows the difference between persons and beasts, and that the spirit or soulish nature of one is immortal (and hence "goes up" to God) while the spirit of the other is not immortal (and hence "goes down" to the grave just as the flesh disintegrates into dust).

The final verse of the chapter reiterates this same rhetorical question. "Who can bring him to see what will happen after him?" From the context the answer is abundantly clear, even if the answer is not immediately verbalized: it is God who will make the final evaluation on life in its totality. Men and women should not live as if God were not to be faced in eternity and as if there were nothing more to mortal humans than their flesh which will turn to dust in the grave just as the flesh of animals will. There is more. The undertaker cannot and does not get everything when he calls for the remains. The spirit has gone already to be with God in the case of those men and women who fear him and who wish to please him.

Therefore, we would translate Ecclesiastes 3:19-21 as follows: For what happens to humanity also happens to the beast; one and the same thing happens to both of them; as the one dies, so the other dies: the same breath is in both of them; there is no advantage [based on this one event of death] of the man over the beast. Both go to one place, that is, the grave. Both are [made out] of the dust and both return to the dust. Who knows the spirit of an individual? He [or she] is the one that goes upward [to God], but the spirit of the beast is the one that goes downward to the earth.

· C H A P T E R 5 4 ·

Do Not Be Overrighteous, Neither Be Overwise

Do not be overrighteous, neither be overwise—why
destroy yourself? Do not be overwicked, and
do not be a fool—why die before your time? It is good to
grasp the one and not to let go of the other.
The man who fears God will avoid all extremes.
ECCLESIASTES 7:16-18

For all too many, Solomon's advice has been labeled as the golden mean. It is as if he had said, "Don't be too holy and don't be an outright criminal; just sin moderately!"

But this reading of these verses is indefensible. The Preacher (as the writer calls himself) is not cautioning against people being goody two shoes or their possessing too much religion or consistency in their faith. There was an altogether different danger which occupies the mind of the writer. It was the danger, not of how men and women are perceived by others, but how men and women perceive themselves. The danger was that individuals might delude themselves through the multiplicity of their pseudoreligious acts which would be nothing more in reality than ostentatious pieces of showmanship in the act of worship and alleged service to God.

The real clue to this passage is to be found in the second verb of verse 16, *to be wise.* This form must be rendered reflexively according to the Hebrew verb form: *to think oneself to be furnished with wisdom.* As such, it makes the same point as the famous text in Proverbs 3:7 does, "Be not wise in your own eyes" (RSV). Thus it was not the case of having too much righteousness or wisdom; rather, it was the problem of self-delusion and the problem of having a super ego that needed to have large doses of humility added. When people become too holy, too righteous and too wise in their own eyes, then they become too holy and too wise for everyone—not in reality, of course; but in their own estimation!

Since verse 17 follows the same pattern set as verse 16, and since the two verses are part of the same thought, the resulting translation would be:

Do not multiply [your] righteousness and do not play the part of the wise [in your own eyes]—why destroy yourself? Do not multiply [your] wickedness and do not be a [downright] fool— why die before your time?

The fact that this interpretation is the correct one can now be tested by its contextual compatibility with verse 18. It is good, urged Solomon, that women and men take hold of "this" (namely, true wisdom that comes from the fear of God and not that which comes from braggadocio), rather than grasping "that" (that is, the folly of fools).

In the end, it is the person who fears God who will be delivered from all these extremes, says verse 18. That is what protects God's people from absurdity. Neither a person's folly, nor their conceited righteousness will serve well as a guide or as a guise to mask the real need of the heart. True wisdom can only be found in coming to fear God.

But no one is ever going to be able to stand before a just and holy God based on a so-called middle way of the golden mean which attempts to counterbalance opposites in moderate doses. Such self-imposed estimates of what God desires are fruitless and to no avail spiritually. In fact, there is no possibility of claiming to have arrived morally while maintaining a middle path based on acting now for virtue and now for vice.

The Preacher, then, is not suggesting something that is immoral; he is, on the contrary, an enemy of false righteousness as well as an exposer of false pretensions to wisdom.

· CHAPTER 55 ·

I Bring Prosperity and I Create Disaster

*I form light and create darkness, I
bring prosperity and create disaster;
I, the LORD, do all these things.*
ISAIAH 45:7

The assertion in this passage is so bold that Marcion, an early Christian merchant who broke with mainstream Christian faith, used this text to prove that the God of the Old Testament was a different being from the God of the New. Thus the nature of this hard saying is simply this: Is God the author of evil?

Numerous texts flatly declare that God is not, and could not be, the author of evil. For example, Deuteronomy 32:4 declares that "his works are perfect and all his ways are just. [He is] a faithful God who does no wrong, upright and just is he." Similarly, Psalm 5:4 notes, "You are not a God who takes pleasure in evil." Consequently, if we read the Bible in its total canonical setting, it would seem that God is without evil or any pretense of evil.

The text in question refers to physical evil. As does Lamentations 3:38, the text contrasts prosperity and adversity. Thus the good is physical goodness and happiness while the adversity, or so-called evil, is physical distress, misfortune and natural evil such as the results of storms or other natural calamities.

Even though much of the physical evil often comes through the hands of wicked men and women, ultimately God permits it. Thus, according to the Hebrew way of speaking, which ignores secondary causation in a way Western thought would never do, whatever God permits must be directly attributed to him, often without noting that secondary and sinful parties were the immediate causes of the physical disaster.

The evil spoken of in this text and similar passages (such as Jer 18:11; Lam 3:38; and Amos 3:6) refers to natural evil and not moral evil. Natural evil is seen in the volcano eruption, plague, earthquake, destructive fire. It is God who must allow (and that is the proper term) these calamities to come. And isn't a God who allows natural disasters thereby morally evil?

To pose the question in this manner is to ask for the origins of evil. Christianity has more than answered the problem of the presence of evil (for that is the whole message of the cross) and the problem of the outcome of evil (for Christ's resurrection demonstrates that God can beat out even the last enemy and greatest evil, death itself). But Christianity's most difficult question is the origin of evil. Why did God ever allow "that stuff" in the first place?

Augustine taught us, however, that evil is not a substance. It is, as it were, a by-product of our freedom, and especially our sin. The effects of that sin did not fall solely on the world of humans. Unfortunately, its debilitating effects hit the whole natural world as well. Nevertheless, it is not as if God can do nothing or that he is just as surprised as we are by natural evil. Any disaster must fall within the sovereign will of God, even though God is not the sponsor or author of that evil. It is at this point that we begin to invade the realms of divine mystery when we attempt to harmonize both of these statements.

What we can be sure of, however, is the fact that God is never, ever, the originator and author of evil. It would be just plain contrary to his whole nature and being as consistently revealed in Scripture.

CHAPTER 56

Where Is He Who Set His Holy Spirit among Them?

Yet they rebelled and grieved his Holy Spirit. So he turned and became their enemy and he himself fought against them. Then his people recalled the days of old, the days of Moses and his people—where is he who brought them through the sea, with the shepherd of his flock? Where is he who set his Holy Spirit among them?

ISAIAH 63:10-11

We are startled to find two explicit references to the Holy Spirit in this Old Testament text. Why would he be mentioned here when the New Testament seems to place his coming after the Son returned to his Father in heaven? That is the key issue before us.

All too frequently interpreters have repeated the traditional adage that the Holy Spirit came on certain Old Testament leaders temporarily, but he did not dwell long-term in people until the New Testament period. But here an Old Testament text clearly teaches that the general class of people "rebelled" and "grieved" the Holy Spirit. The text does not refer only to the leaders; *all* the people were involved in an act which reminds us of the New Testament warning, "Do not grieve the Holy Spirit of God" (Eph 4:30).

Even more amazing, this text appears to contain a reference to all three persons of the Trinity. Verse 9 refers to the Father who shared Israel's distress in Egypt, the wilderness and Canaan. But it was "the angel of his presence" (or "his face") that delivered them (v. 9). This is the One in whom the Father had put his name (Ex 23:20-21). That is tantamount to saying that he had the same nature, essence and authority as the Father. That surely was no ordinary angel. It had to be the second person of the Trinity, the Messiah.

Having referred to the Father and the Son, the passage then mentions the Holy Spirit (vv. 10-11). Yahweh and the angel of his presence (that is to say, Jesus, the Messiah), and the Holy Spirit are distinguished as three persons, but not so that the latter two are altogether different from the first. They, in fact, derive their existence, as we learn from other texts, from the first and are one God, forming a single unity. The Holy Spirit was known to the individual believers in the Old Testament, and they could and did rebel against the Holy Spirit individually just as New Testament believers often did, and as we do today.

But what about texts like John 7:37-39; 14:16-17 and 16:7? Do not these texts teach that the Holy Spirit came for the very first time to indwell believers after Christ had ascended into heaven?

No! Jesus had expected Nicodemus to know of the Holy Spirit's special work in bringing people to belief in the Messiah (Jn 3:5-10). In fact, Jesus was "amazed" that Nicodemus could be a teacher of the Jews and not know this important fact. Even before his death, Jesus sent out the Twelve with the assurance that the Holy Spirit would help them speak (Mt 10:20), just as he likewise promised the Holy Spirit would be with all believers when they were hauled before the judges because of their faith (Lk 12:12).

But the most difficult text is John 14:17. Contrary to the New International Version's translation, the text should read: "You know him, for he lives with [para] you and is [not will be] in you." The Greek para does not denote a fluctuating relationship, for this is the preposition that describes the Father and Son already abiding in them (Jn 14:23). Furthermore, the manuscript evidence is strong for the present tense, is in you, rather than the future tense, will be in you. The present tense appears to be less like a correction than the future tense.

Many will question why Pentecost was necessary if the Holy Spirit was already present to some degree in every Old Testament believer. Pentecost was necessary because the Holy Spirit must have a coming in state, in a solemn and visible manner just as Christ had. In this way all could see and know that the promise-plan of God was being fulfilled. This was the event that Joel had anticipated in Joel 2:28-32. Thus, just as the Holy Spirit had already regenerated and indwelled the Old Testament believers, so now it was necessary that he validate all that had been experienced proleptically in the Old Testament. As Calvary validated the promise of forgiveness of sins realized by all who had believed before that first Good Friday, so Pentecost did the same for all who had experienced the Holy Spirit's wonderful work in the Old Testament.

• CHAPTER 57 •

He Who Dies at a Hundred Will Be Thought a Mere Youth

*Never again will there be in it an infant that lives
but a few days, or an old man who does not live
out his years; he who dies at a hundred will be
thought a mere youth; he who fails to reach a hundred
will be considered accursed.*
ISAIAH 65:20

his strange passage is found within one of the two Old Testament references to the "New Heavens and the New Earth," namely, Isaiah 65:17-25. (The other passage is Is 66:22-24.) Both Peter (2 Pet 3:13) and John (Rev 21:1) must have had the first Isaiah passage in mind, for they borrowed its wording.

The problem comes when we examine Isaiah 65:20-25 in light of what John had to say in the Apocalypse about the New Heavens and the New Earth. In Isaiah 65:20 death is possible, but in Revelation 21:4 death is no longer a feature of that new estate. John assures us that God "will wipe every tear from their eyes. There will be no more death or mourning or crying or pain, for the old order of things has passed away."

John depicts the new order of things in the New Heavens and the New Earth as conditions in which absolute perfection has been reached and where sin, death and sorrow are no more. Jesus mentioned that there would be no begetting of children at that time (Lk 20:36). Why then does Isaiah depict what appears to be the same period of time as one in which death, begetting of children (Is 65:23) and "sinners" are present? True, the power of death may be limited, but the very fact that it is at all present is the embarrassing issue in this text.

The only suggestion that seems to make sense treats verses 20-25 of Isaiah 65 as a distinct subparagraph within the topic of the New Heavens and the New Earth. Verses 17-19 may be paraphrased in this manner, "I will make new heavens and a new earth in which the former troubles will be forgotten, but Jerusalem will not be forgotten. Jerusalem will be completely free of any blemish. Sin may be forgotten, but God's people and the city of Jerusalem will not be forgotten."

Within this subparagraph form, the Jerusalem of Isaiah 65:17-19 pertains to the new Jerusalem of the New Heavens and the New Earth. The Jerusalem of verses 20-25 is the Jerusalem of the millennial kingdom of Christ. Such an interpretation recognizes that the writers of Scripture often arranged their materials in a topical, rather than a chronological order. Other examples of this are the three accounts of our Lord's tempting, which appear in different orders in Matthew, Mark and Luke since each Gospel had a different purpose at the point where the temptations were introduced.

Therefore, in the eternal state in which the New Heavens and the New Earth have arrived, there will be no sin, sorrow and death. But when Christ reigns on earth, just prior to this eternal state, some of these burdens will remain, even if only in limited forms. So unexpected will death be that if people die after only

living one hundred years, they will be regarded as having died as
infants. Isaiah 65:20 breaks the chronological order expected in
the chapter and interjects a related note about Jerusalem during
the millennium.

Almost universally the early church believed Revelation 20:1-
6 to represent a period of time, roughly corresponding to a thousand years, which would begin and conclude with two resurrections (the first of the righteous dead in Christ and the second
resurrection of all the dead) and would be the time when, at the
end of this period, Satan would be loosed for one last fling at
opposing God before being finally and forever vanquished. It is
in this same time period, then, that we would assign the strange
collection of facts stated by Isaiah 65:20-25.

Since the millennium is part of the eternal state it introduces,
"this age" could be expected to overlap with "the age to come."
Thirty times the New Testament uses the dual expressions, *this
age* and *the age to come*. *This age* is the current historical process. But
with our Lord's casting out of the demons (Lk 11:20), and especially with the resurrection of Christ from the dead, "the powers
of the age to come" (Heb 6:5) had already begun and overlapped
this present age's historical process. Thus in the "now" believers
were already experiencing some of the evidences and powers to
be experienced in the "not yet" inbursting of Christ into history
at his Second Coming.

In Isaiah 65:25 the prophet repeats the word from Isaiah 11:6-
9. The description of that age to come closes in verse 25 just as
it had in 11:6-9, with the peace in the world of nature. The new
age promises that the patriarchal measure of life will return,
death will be the anomaly and then no more, and the hostility
between man and some undomesticated animals will be ex-
changed for peace.

Some may argue that the prophet could not have handled such
a sharp distinction between the two periods in the age to come.

We will concede that the prophet may not yet have distinguished and separated these into two separate periods. In the foreshortening of horizons, which was so typical in prophecy, this indeed may have happened. But the resolution here mapped out would have been needed, since death could not have been abolished and continued to exist at one and the same time. That alone would have been enough to suggest that a subplot had developed within the main theme of God's new age to come.

None of His Offspring Will Sit on the Throne of David

"As surely as I live," declares the LORD, "even
if you, Jehoiachin son of Jehoiakim king
of Judah, were a signet ring on my
right hand, I would still pull you off."

This is what the LORD says:
"Record this man as if childless,
a man who will not prosper in his lifetime,
for none of his offspring will prosper,
none will sit on the throne of David
or rule anymore in Judah."
JEREMIAH 22:24, 30

Did Jesus the Messiah come from Jehoiachin's line? If so, how could he claim the throne of David through a line cursed by God?

According to 1 Chronicles 3:16-17, Jehoiachin had seven descendants. These, however, were hauled off into Babylon and there, according to an archaeological finding on a Babylonian tablet in the famous Ishtar Gate, all seven descendants were made eunuchs and rendered unable to bear children. In this manner, Jehoiachin became "as if childless," as no man of his seed prospered, nor did any sit on David's throne.

David's line through his son Solomon abruptly ended. However, the line of David *did* continue through one of Solomon's brothers, Nathan (not to be confused with Nathan the prophet). By the best reconstructions possible from the evidence on hand, Jehoiachin adopted the seven sons of Neri, a descendant of David through Nathan. Neri's son Shealtiel died childless and so his brother Pedaiah performed the duty of levirate marriage (Deut 25:5-10), and as a result Zerubbabel was born.

Accordingly, Zerubbabel, the postexilic governor of Judah during the days of Haggai and Zechariah, was the legal son of Shealtiel, the actual son of Pedaiah, and thus the descendant of David on two counts. 1 Chronicles 3:19 informs us that Zerubbabel was the son of Pedaiah, brother of Shealtiel. Luke's genealogy states that Shealtiel was a descendant of Neri (Lk 3:27).

We conclude, therefore, that Jehoiachin's line did come to an end and that God in his wisdom provided for another branch of David's line to continue the promise made to David which led to the coming of Christ the Messiah.

CHAPTER 59

From the Most High Both Calamities and Good Things Come

*Is it not from the mouth of the Most High
that both calamities and good things come?
Why should any living man complain
when punished for his sins?*
LAMENTATIONS 3:38-39

Once again we face the problem of evil being linked with God as its sponsor or author. This issue comes up repeatedly in Scripture, including Isaiah 45:7 and Amos 3:6. In our text at hand Judah faced the destruction of every clear evidence it ever had that God's promise to the patriarchs and David was valid. Jerusalem and God's own dwelling place, the temple, had been destroyed. Was not God the author of these events? Thus many in Israel reasoned.

An alphabetic acrostic (a means of presenting ideas by beginning each line or group of lines with successive letters of the alphabet) mark verses 37-39 as the strophe unit (that is to say, a poetic paragraph) in which this hard saying occurs.

The preceding strophe, verses 34-36, had formed one long sentence. Each of its three members opened with an infinitive which depended on the main verb that came last in verse 36. Thus the sentence asked the question, Has not the Lord seen the three injustices mentioned in the three infinitives? Indeed, he had! He knew about cruel treatment of war prisoners (v. 34), disregard of basic human rights (v. 35) and malpractice in the halls of justice (v. 36).

Such abuse of prisoners outrages God, as we are also told in Psalm 68:6; 69:33; 107:10-16. Likewise, God is offended when a person is stripped of rights "in the presence of the Most High" (Ps 113:5-6) or receives no justice in the halls of government (Ex 23:6; Deut 16:19; 24:17; Prov 17:23; 18:5).

If our misery and pain come from these sources, then we must be assured that God never approves of such distortions and he has noted the sources of our grief (v. 36). This is the context of our strophe, verses 37-39. Whatever successes evil persons may have are only temporarily permitted by God for his wise purposes.

Verse 37 appears to have Psalm 33:9 in mind, which affirms: "He spoke and it came to be, he commanded, and it stood firm." Thus everything must be permitted by the hand of God. However, woe betide the individual, the institution or the group by which it comes! Though God may permit the temporary success of evil and even use it for his glory, that still does not negate the wicked's responsibility for what they do or how they bring it about.

Accordingly, God used Assyria as the rod of his anger against Israel (Is 10), as he used the Babylonians to chastise Judah later on (Hab 1—2), but he also heaped harsh words on both these foreign nations for the way they did the task. God judged them with a series of woes (see, for example, the end of Hab 2).

Our text, in verse 38, does not contrast good and evil but calamity and good. Furthermore, it does not ascribe these calamities directly to God, but says once again that God must permit them for them to happen. Those claiming this is unfair should look to verse 39, "Why should any living person complain when punished for their sins?" As the theme of this section declares, "Because of the LORD's great love we are not consumed, for his compassions never fail" (v. 22). Thus, the Israelites's very existence bore evidence that God still cared for them.

God, however, is angry with mortals for their sin. This whole question of divine anger has been sharply debated over the centuries. It became known as the debate of divine passability (the quality or aptness in God to feel, suffer or be angry) versus the impassibility of God (the denial of these qualities).

Marcion, a second-century gnostic heretic, demanded that his God be impassible. He found the God of the Old Testament to be a demiurge who was unreconcilable with the God of the New Testament. Marcion's God, however, was incapable of taking offense, never angry, entirely apathetic and free of all affections. Though the early church expelled Marcion and anathematized his doctrines in A.D. 144, the struggle continued over whether God could be angered by sin and unrighteousness.

Our problem with evil, according to the non-Christian philosopher Aristotle, was our desire to avenge the harm done to us. Thus evil came to have a connotation of a "brief madness." Such anger was anger out of control. This theory could never define our Lord's anger or any righteous anger. It was no wonder Aristotle's definition of anger was rejected.

The church father Lactantius wrote a classic treatment on God and anger late in the third Christian century. It was entitled *De Ira Dei*, "The Anger of God." For Lactantius, emotions and passions were not inherently evil if they were controlled. But it *was* evil for someone to be in the presence of evil and not to dislike it or be angered by it. To love the good was by definition to hate the evil. Contrariwise, not to hate the evil was not to love the good.

That is why we affirm that God's anger is never explosive, unreasonable or unexplainable. It is, instead, a firm expression of displeasure with all wickedness and sin. In God, anger is never a ruling force or a ruling passion; it is merely the instrument of his will—an instrument he handles with deftness and care. But however he may use his anger to punish or teach, he will never shut off his compassion to us (Ps 77:9).

CHAPTER 60

I Gave Them Over to Statutes That Were Not Good

*I also gave them over to statutes
that were not good and laws
they could not live by.*
EZEKIEL 20:25

How could a law of God issued to give life to its followers instead cause their deaths? And why would God deliberately admit, as this text appears to make God say, that he gave Israel laws that were not good for them and impossible to live by? Surely this passage qualifies as a hard saying.

Some attempt to explain this text by saying verses 25-26 are the blasphemous words of the people. However, the Lord is clearly the speaker in these verses, not the people.

Neither is verse 25 a reference to verse 11, as many have thought in ancient and modern times. Nor is it an allusion to some aspect of the Mosaic law. Some may attempt to argue that this verse foreshadows Paul's recognition of the intrinsic dead-liness of the law, which he explains in Romans 5:20; 7:13 and Galatians 3:19. Again, I strongly protest! In fact, Paul holds the opposite point of view: he denies that the law which was inher-ently good became evil for some through their disobedience (Rom 7:13). Furthermore, in Ezekiel 20 there is the clear echoing of the sentiment in Leviticus 18:5, "Keep my decrees and laws, for the man who obeys them will live by them. I am the LORD." That same thought is repeated in Ezekiel 20:11, 13 and 21. God's statues were such that men and women were expected to "live in them," not die from them.

Therefore the statutes mentioned in Ezekiel 20:25 cannot be statutes from the Mosaic code, some part of that law, such as the ceremonial law, or even the threats contained there. Certainly God's ceremonial commandments were good and came with promises. And the threats were never called "statutes" or "judg-ments" by Moses.

Verse 26 makes clear what these statutes were. Israel had been defiled by adopting the Canaanite practice of sacrificing their firstborn children to the god Molech. Indeed, there is a quasi-allusion to the commandment given in Exodus 13:12: "You are to give over to the LORD the first offspring of every womb." However, the Israelites perverted the practice by offering the children to Molech instead of dedicating them to the Lord as he had prescribed. Israel also confused their perversions with an-other law of God, Exodus 22:29, "You must give me the firstborn of your sons."

In this manner, God sent them "a powerful delusion" (2 Thess 2:11) and "gave them over to the worship of the heavenly bodies" (Acts 7:42). In a sense, all this was a type of hardening in which all who did not renounce idolatry were given up to its power and control. That is why we find that verse 26 concludes with the dreadful note, "that I might fill them with horror so they would know that I am the LORD."

Isaiah 63:17 asks, "Why, O LORD, do you make us wander from your ways and harden our hearts so we do not revere you?" In the same way, God is said here to have given death-bringing statutes to the Israelites when he saw their perverse behavior toward his ordinances and commandments. To punish their unfaithfulness, he subjected them to influences which accelerated their already clear departure from the truth. They wrongfully thought they were observing the law of God. However, they had so distorted their thinking that they could no longer discern God's law from the law of the pagan land.

Likewise, when Ezekiel 20:26 says "I polluted them in their gifts," or as the New International Version has it, "I let them become defiled through their gifts," this text also speaks as if God himself polluted them so he might return them more quickly to their spiritual senses. Thus in both cases, God's participation is dramatically stated to jar the consciences of a blinded populace. Thus, God identifies himself with the instruments of his wrath and of his providential chastisements as an answer to Israel's sin. Sin became its own punishment (Ps 81:12; Ezek 14:9; Rom 1:24-25).

Without stopping to acknowledge the presence of secondary, and culpable, causes, what God permitted and allowed is directly attributed to him. But on no account was there the least hint that the Mosaic law was to be faulted or judged beyond anyone's ability to live by.

· C H A P T E R 6 1 ·

I Heard,
But I Did
Not Understand

*I heard, but I did not understand. So I asked, "My
Lord, what will the outcome of all this be?"
He replied, "Go your way, Daniel, because the words
are closed up and sealed until the time of the
end. . . . None of the wicked will understand,
but those who are wise will understand."*
DANIEL 12:8-10

Some clumsily attempting to lessen God's revelatory ability and others
trying to heighten the supernatural aspects of Scripture have
argued that the prophets who wrote Scripture often did not
understand what they wrote. Daniel's plain assertion, "I heard,
but I did not understand," is used to prove that prophets often
"spoke better than they knew."

But this conclusion is too simplistic. It fails to ask the question,
What was it that Daniel did not understand? Was it the meaning
of his scriptural writings?

Not at all! The incomprehensible words were not his own, but
those of the angel who had been speaking to him (v. 7). More-

over, the angel's words were never clarified. They were to be
"closed up and sealed until the time of the end." This expression
echoes Isaiah 8:16, "Bind up the testimony and seal up the law."
In both of these texts, the "sealing" of the testimonies referred
to the *certainty* of their predictions, not their mysteriousness or
evasiveness from the prophet to whom they had been disclosed
or unveiled (as the word *revelation* means).

In this case, Daniel's question was a temporal one, "What will
the outcome of all this be?" Daniel wanted to know the state of
affairs at the close of the "time, times and half a time" (Dan 12:7).
But to this question, as with most temporal questions arising
from prophecy, God gives no further disclosure. Even the Son
of Man did not know the time of his own Second Coming.

Failure to know the temporal details of prophecy is hardly a
basis for asserting that "the prophets wrote better than they
knew." Unfortunately this dubious principle has gained wide-
spread popularity. The obvious rejoinder is, "Better than what?"
What could be meant by the term *better*? Since our Lord has disclosed all that can be classified as Scripture, how then could he
know less than he recorded? And if it is argued that this phrase
means that the writers sometimes wrote things down but had
little or no knowledge of what they had said or meant, then I will
counter that a case for automatic or mechanical writing must be
proven. The only biblical cases for mechanical writing are the
Ten Commandments and the writing on the wall during Belshazzar's feast in the book of Daniel. But these cases hardly set
the pattern for all the other texts.

Because the "sealing up" of the prophecy indicated its certainty, not its hiddenness, Daniel was at times overcome by the
meaning of his prophecies. On one occasion he lay sick for days
(Dan 8:27).

We conclude, then, that Daniel knew all but two aspects of the
prophecies revealed to him: (1) the temporal aspects (an exclusion

we share even today and as noted in 1 Peter 1:10-12) and (2) additional information beyond that revealed to him. No prophet claimed omniscience, only an adequate, God-given knowledge of a limited topic of importance.

Let us acknowledge, of course, that we often are better able than the prophets themselves to understand the *implications* of prophecies because we can now see many different streams of history and prophecy coming together. This is similar to one person accurately describing a country he or she has never visited versus another person not only reading this author's account but visiting that country as well. Nevertheless, our historical advantages cannot diminish the value of the original contributions by God's earthly spokesmen.

• C H A P T E R   6 2 •

Go, Take to Yourself an Adulterous Wife

*When the LORD began to speak through Hosea, the
LORD said to him, "Go, take to yourself an adulterous
wife and children of unfaithfulness, because the
land is guilty of the vilest adultery in departing
from the LORD." So he married Gomer daughter
of Diblaim, and she conceived and bore him a son.*

HOSEA 1:2-3

If we were to take this narrative at face value, we assume God was
commanding something which he had already forbidden. Exodus
20:14 had clearly prohibited adultery. Moreover, God had forbidden priests to marry harlots in Leviticus 21:7. If that was God's
will for priests, his will for prophets could hardly be less demanding.

Nevertheless, we are shocked to hear the Almighty commanding Hosea to "Go, take to yourself an adulterous wife." Was this
meant literally?

Several matters must be carefully observed. First is the matter
of Hosea's writing style, which was very pointed, concise and

laconic. In fact, Hosea is so brief and elliptical, at times, that he borders on obscuring several points, since many allusions escape readers unfamiliar with the ancient context.

In the second place, Hosea obviously wrote this text many years after the fact. The phrase, "In the beginning when Yahweh spoke," or as the New International Version has it, "When the Lord began to speak through Hosea," refers back to the time when the prophet began his work. This cryptic notice suggests the story has been foreshortened and the author may leap ahead to tell us what this woman would become, a fact unknown to Hosea but which God, in his foreknowledge and omniscience, could see. This assertion is not as arbitrary as it may first appear, as we will attempt to show.

Let me emphasize that the events described here really took place and are not merely an internal vision or an allegory, as the long list of interpreters have argued. Placing these events in a dream world or making them purely illustrative would not overcome the implied moral problem on God's part.

We assert that Hosea was told by God to marry Gomer, but that she was not a harlot at that time. The telltale signal of this is the figure of speech known as *zeugma*, which occurs whenever one verb is joined to two objects but grammatically refers only to one of them. In this case the *zeugma* involves the double verbs *Go, take to yourself*, a Hebrew idiom for "get married" (Gen 4:19; 6:2; 19:14; Ex 21:10; 34:16; 1 Sam 25:43). However, though these verbs apply only to Gomer, the text links them to the children as well. There is an ellipsis (that is to say, a dropping out) of a third verb which normally would have been inserted before the noun to read, "and *beget* children." Thus the children are given the same odious name (that is, "children of harlotry"—"children of unfaithfulness" [NIV]), even though two were males—apparently being stigmatized because of their mother's unsavory reputation.

The very fact that Gomer "bore *to him* a son" proves that the eldest child was not born out of wedlock of an unknown father through Gomer's loose living (1:3). It is not stated, as it was of the first child, that Gomer bore her next two children "to him." However, since Hosea named them, a function normally left for the father, there is a strong implication that these children are his as well. Thus the evidence would show that the secondary label "children of adulteries" or "unfaithfulness" is given to the children not because they are products of adultery but because of their mother's subsequent activity.

But what about the label put on Gomer? Must we regard her as a soliciting prostitute? No, the term used in the Hebrew text is too restricted to mean that. The Hebrew text does not say *zonah*, as if it were the intensive form. Instead it uses the plural abstract form of the same word, *zenunim*, thus referring to a personal quality and not to an activity!

So distinctive is this abstract plural that it could describe a personal trait that might have been recognizable prior to the marriage, even though it had not shown itself in actual acts of unfaithfulness. Accordingly, the Lord directed Hosea to marry a woman who was imbued with a propensity for sexual liaisons. Gomer, of course, represented Israel, who was frequently depicted as being pure when God first met her though filled with a desire to go off into spiritual whoredoms. This interpretation would explain the "children of whoredoms" as well. The term would refer to Israel's apostasy, not her sexual activity.

This type of construction where the result is put for what appears to be the purpose is common in other writings from Israel. For example, in Isaiah 6:9-12, it first appears that Isaiah must preach in order to blind the eyes of the people and to stop their ears, but this is actually only the result rather than the purpose of his preaching, as Jesus and the apostles later clarified.

We conclude, then, that Hosea's children were not born out of wedlock from adulterous unions and that Hosea was unaware of what God discerned in the heart of Gomer, that she had an adulterous predisposition and a bent toward sexual promiscuity. Had Hosea married her with the full knowledge of her immorality, he would have had no right to complain later on and put her away. Instead, we contend that none of this was known prior to the marriage or during her childbearing years.

It was this same woman about whom the Lord told Hosea to "Go, show your love to your wife again" (in Hebrew the word *again* goes with the verb *go*, according to the ancient suggested punctuation of the Hebrew Massoretes, and not with the verb *The Lord said)* in Hosea 3:1. It is for this reason that the book of Hosea has been called the Gospel of John of the Old Testament and the book that shows the heart and holiness of God. The apostasying Israelites were just as undeserving as Gomer was.

In conclusion, our hard saying must be understood to be a combination statement. It contains the original command (perhaps something like, "Go, take to yourself a wife and [beget] children") and inserted additions reflecting a later perspective. To sort out the two meanings combined in the verse, we will place square brackets around the additions to show they were not technically part of the original command but were later revealed as the divine reason God chose this wife for Hosea and allowed Hosea to go through such a trying experience. Accordingly, the verse would read: "Go, take to yourself a[n adulterous] wife and (beget) children [of unfaithfulness, because the land is guilty of the vilest adultery in departing from the LORD.]" Thus the earlier divine command was combined with the subsequent realization of his wife's moral lapses. When fitted together, both word and deed, they constituted the total claim and call of God on Hosea's life.

· C H A P T E R 6 3 ·

Where, O Death, Are Your Plagues? Where, O Grave, Is Your Destruction?

I will ransom them from the power of the grave;
I will redeem them from death.
Where, O death, are your plagues?
Where, O grave, is your destruction?
HOSEA 13:14

This text is either one of the greatest notes of triumph over death in the Old Testament, or, by beginning with a rhetorical question which assumes a no answer, it surrenders the helpless to all the weapons of death. Which is true: the first view with its long history of translations going all the way back to the the Greek Septuagint, or the second view which shows up in such modern translations as the Revised Standard Version ("Shall I redeem them from Death? O Death, where are your plagues?"), The New English Bible ("Shall I ransom him from death? Oh, for your plagues, O death!") and Today's English Version or Good News for Modern Man ("Bring on your plagues, death!")?

The first part of this verse has no sign of an interrogative, and therefore we would understand it as one of the most beautiful gospel promises in the Old Testament. The Lord, who spoke in verses 4-11 of this chapter, is the speaker of this verse, not Hosea. Our Lord affirms that he will ransom and redeem Israel from the grip of death and the grave. *To ransom* means to buy the freedom of a person by paying the stipulated price for such a deliverance. The opening couplet gives a ringing challenge that makes it a straightforward promise. Our God will deliver mankind by fulfilling the law (Mt 3:15), removing the guilt (Jn 1:29) and personally suffering the penalties due to mankind for their sin (Jn 3:16).

How then shall we translate it? "*Where*, O death . . . ?" and "Where, O grave . . . ?" or "*I will be* your plagues, O death . . ." and "*I will be* your destruction, O grave." Normally the translation which denotes permission, as in *I will be* is restricted to the second- and third-person pronouns (*you* and *he/she*) forms; however, the first-person Hebrew jussive form does occur in some exceptional cases.

But verse 10 of this chapter had just translated this same Hebrew word as *where*. That would seem to settle the matter even though verse 10 has an added Hebrew adverb in this same expression. The form probably reflects Hosea's special northern dialect.

But some protest that a promise of redemption is incompatible with the threats pronounced in verses 7-13 and repeated in verses 15-16. The complaint charges that this promise in verse 14 is surrounded contextually with curses and judgments.

The answer, of course, is that the same situation is found in Genesis 3:15. It too is surrounded with the curses on the woman, the serpent, the man, and the ground (Gen 3:8-14; 16-19). Often God will interject this note of hope right in the midst of humanity's darkest moments and most deserved judgments.

Therefore, the taunt song to death and the grave is the most appropriate rendering of the last part of verse 14. It is this same paean that the apostle Paul will raise in 1 Corinthians 15:55. It only asks in mocking tones what the first part of verse 14 had clearly affirmed as a statement: God can and will ransom them from the power of the grave. He can deliver them even after death has done its worst. No wonder the prophet cries out with such triumphant glee and says (after a manner of speaking): "Come on, death, let's see your stuff now! Come on, grave, put up your fists and fight!"

So certain is this affirmation that even God himself can see no cause or condition for changing his mind or intentions. He will have no repentance, says the end of verse 14. There will be no regrets or remorse over this decision in the divine mind, for God has spoken and that will be that.

CHAPTER 64

The Day
of the Lord
Is Near

Alas for that day!
For the day of the LORD is near;
it will come like destruction from the Almighty.
JOEL 1:15

What will this day of the Lord be like? And how can Joel say it
is near or imminent when five different prophets in four different centuries (the latter ones aware of the earlier ones) declared
that it was just that—near? If it were so near, why hadn't it
happened in over four hundred years?

Ten times the prophets warned that that day was near (Joel
1:15; 2:1; 3:14; Obad 15; Is 13:6; Zeph 1:7, 14 [twice]; Ezek 30:3
[twice]). But these prophets, most likely in this chronological
order, ministered in the ninth century B.C. (probably, but not
with total certainty, Joel and Obadiah), the eighth century (Isaiah), the seventh century (Zephaniah), and the sixth century

(Ezekiel). Yet each repeatedly warned that that day of the Lord was imminent and certain to come. They even gave their contemporaries instances of what impact it would have on people and the nations. But they always reserved the worst and final fulfillment for the future.

The day of the Lord is much too complex a subject to be contained in a brief discussion, for the prophets found it a most engaging topic in their ministries and writings. But it does not completely defy description. It will be a time when God judges the wicked as never before and simultaneously completes the salvation and deliverance of the redeemed.

The Lord will come to "judge the world" (Ps 9:8; 96:13; 98:9). In that day, "The LORD will be king over the whole earth. On that day there will be one LORD, and his name the only name" (Zech 14:9).

It will also be a day of theophany or the appearance of God. He will appear on the Mount of Olives, just where the Son of God told the men from Galilee that he would come again in like manner as they had seen him go (Zech 14:3-4). When he appears, Jerusalem will be attacked and he personally will lead his people against the nations that have gathered there to settle the Jewish question once and for all (Zech 14: 3-12; Joel 3).

Because of this insurrection against the Lord and his cause, Amos describes this day as one of darkness and mourning (Amos 5:18-20) for those who had only the popular concept that the Messiah would return to magically right all wrongs for everyone, regardless of the person's personal belief in him. Amos went on to show how false this hope was.

In the New Testament this day is still being discussed. It is known as *that day* (Mt 7:22; 1 Thess 5:4), the *day of God* (2 Pet 3:12), the *day of wrath* (Rom 2:5-6), and the *day of our Lord Jesus Christ* (2 Cor 1:14; Phil 1:6, 10). It had the same foreboding aspect of horrors for the unbeliever, yet it was a bright day of release and joy for all who looked forward to Christ's coming.

But this day always had an impending nature to it. Though it found partial fulfillment in such events as Joel's locust plagues, the destruction of Jerusalem and the threat of national invasions, its final and climactic fulfillment always remained in Christ's future return.

Therefore, the *day of the Lord* was a term rich in content. It marked off a divinely inaugurated future period, which already had in some sense begun with the ongoing history of the kingdom of God. In such a blend of history and prophecy, the prophet's promise that that day was coming in the eschatological (Last Days) setting was reinforced by God's present-day foreshadowings of what was to come. This would induce men and women to repent and to prepare for that day. Its blessings would extend to a new Jerusalem, the endowment of the Holy Spirit in a unique way and the cleansing and purification of all that needed it.

When this came, the kingdom would be the Lord's and all other rivalries would cease—forever!

• C H A P T E R 6 5 •

Act Justly, Love Mercy and Walk Humbly with Your God

With what shall I come before the LORD
and bow down before the exalted God?
Shall I come before him with burnt offerings,
with calves a year old?
Will the LORD be pleased with thousands of rams,
with ten thousand rivers of oil?
Shall I offer my firstborn for my transgression,
the fruit of my body for the sin of my soul?
He has showed you, O man, what is good.
And what does the LORD require of you?
To act justly and to love mercy
and to walk humbly with your God.
MICAH 6:6-8

Two different and opposing kinds of false claims are made about this text. Some readers see the text refuting all external, ceremonial religion in favor of a totally internalized faith response to God. Others, reacting against more conservative theologies of the atonement, argue that essential religious acts focus solely on issues of justice, mercy and humility; all else is beyond what even God expects of the most devout.

Unfortunately, both positions are extremes that fail to grasp the prophet Micah's point. His answer to the question, "With what [things] shall I come before the Lord?" certainly went beyond the people's appalling response. They were convinced that they could earn God's favor by deeds and various types of religious and even pagan acts, such as the human sacrifice of their oldest child. They were ready to bargain with God and to bid high if need be. But their quasi-self-righteousness availed them nothing in God's sight.

The prophet's answer, on behalf of his Lord, was very different from theirs, though it was hardly novel. They had already known what was good and pleasing to God, because God had revealed it time and time again. Each time they had refused to acknowledge it as God's way.

Three items are mentioned: justice, mercy and humility before God. The norm of justice had been set by the character and person of the Living God, not by human standards. God's norm of justice, announced in his law, demanded perfect righteousness available only by faith in the God who had promised to send the seed of promise.

Mercy, the second demand, should be patterned after God's mercy as defined in his Word—an unselfish love toward God and one's neighbor.

The third was a call for the people to remember that any good found in them was due to the Lord's enabling. Those claiming the Lord as their God were to prove it by a godly lifestyle. Pride was the antithesis of what was required here: faith. To walk humbly was to live by faith. Such faith sought to give God first place instead of usurping it for oneself. In our Lord's use of this passage in Matthew 23:23, he listed the three requisites for pleasing God as "justice, mercy and faithfulness."

Thus, this passage is more than just an ethical or cultic substitute for all inventions of religion posed by mortals. It is duty, indeed, but duty grounded in the character and grace of God. The question asked in Micah 6:6 is very similar to the question posed in Deuteronomy 10:12, "And now, O Israel, what does the LORD your God ask of you?" But the background for both questions is the same, for in Deuteronomy 10, as here in Micah 6, God had announced himself ready to destroy Israel for their disobedience in the golden-calf episode had not Moses, prepared by God for such an occasion, interceded on their behalf and turned the judgment of God away.

Thus this saying is not an invitation, in lieu of the gospel, to save oneself by kindly acts of equity and fairness. Nor is it an attack on the forms of sacrifices and cultic acts mentioned in the tabernacle and temple instructions. It was instead a call for the natural consequence of truly forgiven men and women to demonstrate the reality of their faith by living it out in the marketplace. Such living would be accompanied with acts and deeds of mercy, justice and giving of oneself for the orphan, the widow and the poor.

• CHAPTER 66 •

The Lord Is a Jealous and Avenging God

The LORD is a jealous and avenging God;
the LORD takes vengeance and is filled with wrath.
The LORD takes vengeance on his foes
and maintains his wrath against his enemies.
The LORD is slow to anger and great in power;
the LORD will not leave the guilty unpunished.
NAHUM 1:2-3

T he declaration of Exodus 34:6, which appears to assure us that God is not jealous, is repeated ten times in the Old Testament: "The LORD, the LORD, the compassionate and gracious God, slow to anger, abounding in love and faithfulness, maintaining love to thousands, and forgiving wickedness, rebellion and sin."

Other texts, however, appear to assert that God is indeed jealous. Exodus 20:5 clearly states, "I, the LORD your God, am a jealous God." Deuteronomy 29:20 reiterates, "The LORD will never be willing to forgive [the person who invokes God's blessing on himself and goes his own way thinking it is safe to do as he or she pleases]; his wrath and zeal [jealousy] will burn against that man." Psalm 78:58 asserts, "They angered him with their high places; they aroused his jealousy with their idols." Ezekiel 36:5 confirms, "This is what the Sovereign LORD says: In my burning zeal [or jealousy] I have spoken against the rest of the nations and against all Edom, for with glee and with malice in their hearts they made my land their own possession so that they might plunder its pastureland." So which set of texts is correct and how are we to understand God? Is he jealous and filled with envy or is he not?

The anthropopathic descriptions of God (which describe God's emotions in human terms) help us understand that God is not just an abstract idea but a living and active person. He does have emotions similar to our human emotions of jealousy, vengeance, anger, patience and goodness—with the exception that none of these are tainted with sin.

Certainly God has many agreeable traits, as Nahum 1:7 goes on to affirm: "The Lord is good. . . . He cares for those who trust in him." In Nahum 1:3 God is also described as being "slow to anger and great in power." But what of his seemingly less attractive emotions?

God's jealousy is often linked in Scripture with his anger. As such, it is an expression of his holiness: "I will be zealous [or jealous] for my holy name" (Ezek 39:25). But in no sense is his jealousy or zeal explosive or irrational. Those depicting the God of the Old Testament as having a mysterious, if not primal force, which could break out against any of his creatures at any time for any or no reason have an overly active scholarly or lay imagination. Never does God's zeal or wrath border on caprice or the demonic.

God's wrath is indeed a terrible reality in both testaments, but it always reflects a totally consistent personality which cannot abide the presence of sin. God's anger never causes God to avenge himself or retaliate, as if he were briefly insane. In our

Lord, anger may be defined as his arousing himself to act against sin.

The same could be said about the word translated *vengeance* in the hard saying at hand. Divine vengeance can only be understood in the light of the Old Testament's teaching on the holiness and justice of God. Of the seventy-eight times this word is used in the Old Testament, fifty-one involve situations where God is the perpetrator. The classical text is Deuteronomy 32:35, "It is mine to avenge; I will repay." God cannot be God if he allows sin and rebellion to go unpunished. His very character cries out for the opposite.

Basically, there are two ways in which God takes vengeance: (1) he becomes the champion of the cause of those oppressed by the enemy (Ps 94); and (2) he punishes those who break covenant with him (Lev 26:24-25).

If the book of Nahum appears to exhibit savage joy over the crushing defeat of the Assyrian capital, Nineveh, the question must arise: When is one justified in rejoicing over the downfall of a despotic and tyrannical nation? If the answer is that one must wait until the rejoicing nation has been purged of their own sins, then we should be careful in our smugness over the destruction of Nazi Germany. Our own purging may lie ahead.

Contrary to the popular criticism of the book of Nahum, Nahum's condemnation of Nineveh grows out of a moral and ethical concept of God. In the prophet's thought, God is sovereign Lord over the whole creation, including all the nations. As a holy God, he abhors any form of unrighteousness, but all the more when it is committed on an international scale.

There are three basic reasons why God decreed the end of the Assyrian empire. First, the Assyrians not only opposed Israel, they opposed God (Nahum 1:9, 11, 14). Second, they flouted the law and moral order of God. In her cavalier manner, Assyria drew not only her own citizens into the dragnet, but she also lured many other nations into her practices, just as a harlot lures her prey to destruction (Nahum 2:13; 3:4). Finally, Assyria's imperial greed provoked robberies and wrongs of every sort.

God, therefore, does not indifferently and helplessly observe the sins of the nations multiply. Instead, he is a warmhearted, understanding, but thoroughly just and righteous God who will act against those who persist in flouting everything he is and stands for. The fact that God expresses jealousy, vengeance or wrath is a sign that he cares for his people and champions their cause. He can and he will administer justice with equity among the nations.

The words *jealousy*—or as it is more accurately rendered when referring to God, *zeal*—and *vengeance* may both be used in a good and a bad sense. When applied to God, they denote that God is intensely concerned for his own character and reputation. Thus, everything that ultimately threatens his honor, esteem and reverence, may be regarded as the object of his jealousy and vengeance. The metaphor best depicting this emotion is that of the jealous husband, which God is said to be when false gods and false allegiances play the parts of suitors and potential paramours. He cannot and will not tolerate rivalry of any kind—our spiritual lives depend on his tenacious hold on us.

CHAPTER 67

Though the Fig Tree Does Not Bud, Yet I Will Rejoice in the Lord

I heard and my heart pounded,
my lips quivered at the sound;
decay crept into my bones,
and my legs trembled.
Yet I will wait patiently for the day of calamity
to come on the nation invading us.
Though the fig tree does not bud
and there are no grapes on the vines,
though the olive crop fails
and the fields produce no food,
though there are no sheep in the pen
and no cattle in the stalls,
yet I will rejoice in the LORD,
I will be joyful in God my Savior.
HABAKKUK 3:16-18

The prophet Habakkuk had been given a vision which left him deeply agitated. He was so shaken by the terrifying news that God would bring the Babylonian hordes down on Judah that his body seemed to fall to pieces right then and there. There can be no doubt that the prophet experienced real fear with pronounced physical and psychological effects.

The amazing aspect of this saying, and the fact that makes it so noteworthy, is that in spite of all of the trauma, Habakkuk received the gift of joy. This was not merely resignation about things over which he had no control. The prophet wasn't saying, "Let's make the best of it; one thing is for sure, you can't fight city hall."

Instead, this text teaches us to rejoice in God even when every instinct in our bodies is crying out with grief. Though fully alarmed at the outrage that would take place, Habakkuk experienced a holy joy, a divine enabling to rejoice in the Lord.

The object of his joy was the God of his salvation. Some things are just more abiding and important than this temporal world. Sometimes it seems as if history is out of control and no one knows where it all will end. Since God is ultimately behind the course of history, he is in control and *he* knows where it will end.

Thus, all the symbols of prosperity (the fig tree, the vine, the olive, the fields, the flocks and the herds of cattle) of verse 17 could be removed, but none of these compared with the joy that came from the living God himself. Even though that joy did not in itself mitigate the depth of the physical pain felt in the body, it did transcend it in worth, reality and depth.

This text has enormous relevance for a Christian view of history and for those who are oppressed and experiencing the reality of the conqueror's or enemy's wrath.

· C H A P T E R 6 8 ·

The Desired
of All Nations
Will Come

This is what the LORD Almighty says:
"In a little while I will once more shake
the heavens and the earth, the sea and the dry land.
I will shake all nations, and the desired of
all nations will come, and I will fill this
house with glory," says the LORD Almighty.
HAGGAI 2:6-7

T*he translation "Desire of all nations" in Haggai 2:7 has taken such*
deep root, through its use in sermons, Christmas hymns and a
long history of Jewish and Christian commentary, that it is difficult to handle this text as objectively as we should.

The King James rendering, "The desire of all nations shall
come," has been challenged by almost every modern translation
in English. The 1901 American Standard Version changed *desire*
to *precious things*, while the New American Standard Bible now
reads, "They will come with the wealth of all nations." The New
English Bible has, "The treasure of all nations shall come hither,"
and the New American Bible uses the word *treasures*. Clearly, the

trend is away from giving the word *desire* a Messianic connotation, favoring instead the impersonal idea of "valuables" or "desired things."

All the controversy stems from the use of the singular feminine noun, *desire*, with a plural verb, *[they] come*. As soon as this
is pointed out, the modern commentators drop any further
search or references to a person and assume that the noun must
be plural since the verb is.

Actually, both the singular and plural forms of this Hebrew
noun, *hemdat*, translated *desire* are used in the Old Testament to
refer to persons. Saul was described as being "the desire of all
Israel" in 1 Samuel 9:20. Likewise Daniel 11:37 includes, "the one
desired by women." The plural form of the same word appears
three times to refer to Daniel himself in Daniel 9:23 and 10:11,
19. In these cases, the word is usually translated as "highly es-
teemed" and a "man of high esteem" (*'ish hamudoth*).

Of course this same word is also used to describe valuable
possessions, especially silver and gold. In this construction, the
emphasis usually falls on the preciousness of the items.

Which is correct, then? Did Haggai intend to talk about the
valuables that the Gentiles would bring, or did he intend to refer
to the Messiah himself, as most of the ancient commentaries and
the Vulgate had it?

Those opting for a reference to precious gifts believe this
rendering makes contextual sense. The precious gifts would
compensate for the temple's lack of adornment. Accordingly, the
Gentiles would come laden down with gifts for the temple out
of homage to the Lord of the earth, a foretaste of the good things
to come in the New Covenant. This interpretation is said to
square with the plural verb and the feminine singular subject.

However, the earliest Jewish interpretation and the majority
of early Christian interpreters referred this passage to the Messiah. Since the word *desire* is used to refer to a person in several

key passages, and since there is a longing of all the nations for a deliverer, acknowledged or not, it seems fair to understand this passage as a reference to the Messiah, our Lord Jesus Christ. Hebrew often places the concrete word for an abstract noun. Nor should we be thrown off balance by the presence of a plural verb, for often when one verb is controlled by two nouns, the verb agrees with the second noun even if the verb actually belongs with the former substantive.

Although some are reluctant to adopt a Messianic interpretation, the word *desire* can be treated as an accusative—a construction which is frequently adopted with verbs of motion: "And they will come to the desire of all nations [namely, Christ]." This rendering avoids the problem of the plural verb *come*, as was first suggested by Cocceius.

In accordance with a Messianic interpretation, just as the first temple was filled with the glory of God, so this temple will yet be filled with the divine glory in Christ (Jn 1:14), a glory which shall be revealed at the Second Coming of Christ (Mal 3:1).

• C H A P T E R 6 9 •

The Man Whose Name Is Branch Will Be a Priest on His Throne

Tell [Joshua, the High Priest] this is what the LORD Almighty says: "Here is the man whose name is the Branch, and he will branch out from his place and build the temple of the LORD. It is he who will build the temple of the LORD, and he will be clothed with majesty and will sit and rule on his throne. And he will be a priest on his throne. And there will be harmony between the two."

ZECHARIAH 6:12-13

Who is this one who is called the Branch and who seems to possess the office and authority of both priest and king? Is this a Messianic passage, or does it refer to a postexilic prophet?

When the Babylonian captives heard the temple was being rebuilt, they sent a delegation of three men with a gift for the temple. The Lord, pleased with the exiles' response, instructed the prophet to make the gift of silver and gold into a crown and to place it on the head of Joshua, the high priest. Although the action was merely symbolic, such transference of the royal crown from the tribe of Judah to the tribe of Levi must have met with surprise. Had God not promised in Genesis 49:10-12 that the privilege of reigning would be vested in the tribe of Judah? And would not the coming Messiah King come from David's line (2 Sam 7:12-20)?

Many unbelieving modern scholars attempt to harmonize these facts by substituting the name *Zerubbabel* (the Davidic descendant and governor of Judah at the time) for the name *Joshua*. But the Lord himself reveals the interpretation of this symbolic act in verses 12-15.

It is clear that the term *Branch* is a Messianic term, for under this title four different aspects of his character are presented in four major teaching passages: He is the king (Jer 23:5-6), the servant (Zech 3:8), the man (Zech 6:12) and the Branch of Yahweh (Is 4:2). Indeed, many have noted how this fourfold picture of the Messiah corresponds to the fourfold picture of the historical Christ in the four Gospels of the New Testament.

This prophecy promises four particulars regarding the Messiah's character and rule: (1) "He will be a priest on his throne"; (2) "He will build the temple of the LORD"; (3) "He will be clothed with majesty and will sit and rule on his throne"; and (4) "Those who are far off [Gentiles] will come and build the temple of the Lord."

It is easy to identify these features with the character and the program of Jesus of Nazareth. He is represented as the High Priest and as King in the New Testament. It is also true that Gentiles, those who were "afar off" (Acts 2:39; Eph 2:13), will come in the end time and acknowledge his dignity.

Accordingly, there is perfect harmony and accord between the two offices of Priest and King in the Messiah—"harmony between the two" (Zech 6:13). The Messiah as Priest-King will produce peace because he will personally hold both the administrative and judicial functions: the ecclesiastical and spiritual ones combined! He becomes our peace.

The crowning of the high priest in the temple of the Lord was to be a reminder concerning the coming union of the King and Priest in one person, the Messiah. Such princely gifts coming from the far-off Babylonian exiles was but a harbinger and precursor of the wealth of the nations which would pour into Jerusalem when Messiah the Branch would be received as King of kings and Lord of lords.

• C H A P T E R 7 0 •

So They Paid
Me Thirty Pieces
of Silver

*I told them, "If you think it best, give me my pay; but
if not, keep it." So they paid me thirty pieces
of silver. And the LORD said to me, "Throw it to the
potter"—the handsome price at which they priced me!
So I took the thirty pieces of silver and threw them into the
house of the LORD to the potter.*
ZECHARIAH 11:12-13

Two difficulties appear when Zechariah's prophetic actions are
compared with their fulfillment recorded in Matthew 27:7-10.
First, certain details of Zechariah's prophetic symbolism do not
seem to fit the historical account. Second, Matthew ascribes
these words to Jeremiah, but he clearly is quoting Zechariah.
How shall we resolve these matters?

Zechariah's prophetic parable followed his prophecy of the
Good Shepherd's relations to the flock. In verse 11 the people
reacted to Zechariah's breaking his staff. They realized that God
was annulling the covenant of protection over them. Some terrible acts of judgment were ahead!

In verse 12 the prophet requested payment for his services and for alerting the people. He posed his request delicately, assuming that they might not wish to pay him because they had treated their Shepherd so contemptibly. In effect, he said, "If you don't care to pay me, fine; don't bother!" However, the people did not realize that Zechariah's abrupt termination of his pastoral role reflected more their own abandonment of their Shepherd than his choice to end his service.

Their reply insulted him and the cause he represented. They paid him thirty pieces of silver, the same price fetched by a slave gored by an ox (Ex 21:32). Zechariah, here impersonating the Messiah, was then advised to take this most "handsome!" (surely said in irony and sarcasm) price and cast it to the potter in the house of the Lord. The expression *to cast it to the potter* usually was an idiomatic proverb approximately meaning, "throw it to the dogs," or "get rid of it." But its connection with the house of the Lord makes that solution unlikely. Moreover, it is doubtful that the potter would have been in the house of the Lord. Rather, this phrase could be a cryptic description of his casting the money into the temple where it was taken up and used to purchase a field of the potter, since tainted money was unwelcome in the temple (Deut 23:18).

But what of Matthew's use of this acted-out parable? Matthew probably attributed the text to Jeremiah because Jeremiah, in many Hebrew manuscripts, headed up the collection of the prophets and his name was used to designate all in the collection. Our book titles with their chapter and verse divisions are a fairly recent innovation. Also Matthew may have attributed this quotation to Jeremiah because this text was paired with Jeremiah 18:1-4; 32:6-9. Thus he cited the name of the better-known and more prominent prophet. In fact, not one of the four other places where the New Testament quotes from Zechariah does it mention his name (Mt 21:4-5; 26:31; Jn 12:14; 19:37).

On the second problem, Matthew's use of this text, we counter by arguing that the New Testament citings of the Old very much agree with the meaning found in the Old Testament. Judas did receive thirty pieces of silver for betraying Jesus of Nazareth. Because these wages represented blood money, with stricken conscience Judas took the money and threw it into the temple. However, because this money was unfit for temple service, it was used to buy a potter's field as a burial place for strangers (Mt 27:6-10).

Certainly, these actions follow the pattern set by the prophet, even though there are a few slight differences such as *I threw* being rendered in the Gospel as *and they gave them* (Mt 27:10), and *I took the thirty pieces of silver* becoming *and they took the thirty pieces of silver* (Mt 27:9), and *at which they priced me* becoming *the price set on him by the people of Israel* (Mt 27:9). But these changes are required by the position of the narrator, his use of his own tenses and the place where he introduced this text into his story.

Zechariah, we may conclude, accurately saw the tragic events connected with the betrayal of our Lord and warned Judah long before the events took place. What a fantastic prophecy!

CHAPTER 71

I Have Loved Jacob, But Esau I Have Hated

*"I have loved you," says the LORD. "But you ask,
'How have you loved us?' Was not Esau Jacob's
brother?" the LORD says. "Yet I have loved Jacob, but Esau
I have hated, and I have turned his mountains into a
wasteland and left his inheritance to the desert jackals."*
MALACHI 1:2-3

If God is depicted as being good to all (Ps 145:9), how can he hate Esau? Surely this runs counter to all we know about the God and Father of our Lord Jesus Christ.

With his usual abruptness, Malachi announces his message succinctly enough to please even the most impatient listener. It was simply this: "I have loved you."

Typical for this crowd, as Malachi reported, they answered back in that incredulous tone of unbelief, "Who? Us? God has loved us? Since when?" This, then, became the basis for the contrast which now had to be drawn between Jacob and Esau, two brothers who represented two different ways that God works.

God's election love illustrates how God can claim to love Jacob. Both Esau and Jacob were the sons of that man of promise, Isaac. However, even though Esau was the firstborn, God chose Jacob, emphasizing that his grace had nothing to do with natural rights or works. From Esau came the nation of Edom, and from Jacob came the nation of Israel. It is said that God hates Edom and loves Israel. Why?

When Scripture talks about God's hatred, it uses a distinctly biblical idiom which does not imply that Yahweh exhibits disgust, disdain and a desire for revenge. There are clear objects meriting God's hatred, including the seven evils of Proverbs 6:16-19, all forms of hypocritical worship (Is 1:14; Amos 5:21) and even death itself, as Jesus demonstrated at the grave of Lazarus in John 11:33, 38 (see also Mk 3:5; 10:14; and Jn 2:17). Hate can be a proper emotion for disavowing and for expressing antipathy for all that stands against God and his righteous standards. Only one who has truly loved can experience burning anger against all that is wrong and evil.

But in this antonymic pair of *love* and *hate*, as used in Scripture, there is a specialized meaning. A close parallel to the emotions expressed for Jacob and Esau is Jacob's response to his wives, Rachel and Leah, in Genesis 29:30-33. While verses 31 and 33 say that Jacob hated Leah, verse 30 clarifies this usage by stating in the same context that he loved Rachel *more than* Leah. A similar situation is found in Deuteronomy 21:15-17.

To summarize, the hated one is the one *loved less*. The New Testament uses the same terminology in Matthew 6:24 and Luke 16:13. There are two parallel lists which use the formula even more dramatically. Matthew 10:37 says, "Anyone who loves . . . more than me," while Luke 14:26 states the same concept as, "If anyone comes to me and does not hate . . ."

God does not experience psychological hatred with all its negative and sinful connotations. In this text, he merely affirms that

Jacob had had a distinctive call, for when he had been blessed, all the nations of the world would eventually, if not immediately, profit from his blessing. Thus, there came a ranking and a preference, in order to carry out God's plan and to bring the very grace that Esau would also need.

God's love and hate (in his deciding to prefer one person for a certain blessed task) was bestowed apart from anything these men were or did. God's choice of Jacob took place before Jacob's birth (Gen 25:23; Rom 9:11). Thus, it is unfair to interpret these verses as evidence of favoritism or of partiality on the part of God. They express a different set of realities than what our English words generally signify.

CHAPTER 72

In Every Place Incense and Pure Offerings Will Be Brought

"My name will be great among the nations, from
the rising to the setting of the sun. In every
place incense and pure offerings will be
brought to my name, because my name will be great
among the nations," says the LORD Almighty.
MALACHI 1:11

Malachi *has the ability to startle and shock both his audience and* readers as few prophets can. Malachi 1:11 is just one such example. In the midst of an otherwise dull recital of the priests' sins, Malachi interrupted this wearisome affair by announcing that God would indeed triumph with or without the obedience of those entrusted with the nation's spiritual care. But Malachi's outburst of good news was so shocking that many have found this passage a hard saying indeed.

Malachi meant his words to startle, for he began them in verse 11 with a Hebrew word that is almost a shout of joy like "Yes, indeed!" This truth would be so unexpected, transcending as it did the paltry service and heartless attitudes of the priesthood, that it was necessary for Malachi to awaken the reader before introducing a whole new concept.

The new wave of excitement heightened when Malachi foretold that God's name would be exalted by Gentiles worldwide. Though Israel's spiritual leaders despised and demeaned the Lord's great name, that did not mean God was stuck with these worshipers or his cause was at an impasse. God could, and would, raise up true worshipers to his name from all the nations of the world. His cause and his great name would succeed. God was not saddled with Israel just as he is not saddled with any contemporary group of Christians.

The geographical, political and ethnic scope of this promise is set forth in even more startling tones. Clearly, the text affirms that it will be from "the rising to the setting of the sun." The sweep of God's success from East to West reaffirmed the state of affairs noted in 1:5, "Great is the LORD—even beyond the borders of Israel!"

Furthermore, incense and offerings, in fact "pure" offerings, will be offered up "in every place." That must have shaken all those who remembered that only in Jerusalem were they to offer sacrifices and burnt incense before God. In the terms of Leviticus 11 and Deuteronomy 14:3-19, an offering was pure when an unblemished animal was offered as the law prescribed. But the word for *without blemish* was not used here; it was the word that involved one's moral and physical purity as well as ceremonial purity.

That raised the question of how the nations (indeed, Gentiles!) could offer a pure offering in places other than Jerusalem. This could only be possible in a day yet unseen when the good news would reach beyond the borders known to Malachi's audience.

The term *incense* referred, no doubt, to the altar of incense with its symbolic sweet aroma of the saints' prayers constantly rising to God. But this incense would no longer emanate from the temple alone; it would be offered "in every place."

Some try to say this verse refers only to the Jews of the Dispersion or to gentile proselytes. This is only partially true, for it hardly embraces all the terms and conditions of Malachi's text. The Jewish Diaspora and the gentile proselytes signaled just the first fruits of the harvest that was to come in the Messianic age. Moreover, the fact that offerings would be offered worldwide indicated something bigger and newer than what Israel had ever seen or imagined. No wonder Malachi exclaimed, "My name will be great among the nations." The middle wall of partition had been destroyed (Eph 2:14) and God's kingdom had been announced over all the earth.

CHAPTER 73

I
Hate
Divorce

"I hate divorce," says the LORD God of
Israel, "and I hate a man's covering himself
with violence as well as with his
garment," says the LORD Almighty.
MALACHI 2:16

In all Scripture, Malachi 2:16 is at once one of the most succinct and most contested statements on the permanence of marriage. The difficulty comes, in part, from the Hebrew text, which some have pronounced the most obscure in the Old Testament. Further problems come from trying to fathom the Old Testament's position on marriage and divorce. All too many have wrongly assumed that Malachi voiced an opinion that contradicts earlier statements in Scripture.

The section opens with a double question which amounts to a double premise: (1) all Israel has one Father—God; and (2) God created that nation (v. 10). Sadly, however, the population was dealing treacherously with each other and thereby profaning the covenant God had made with their fathers. Malachi 2:10-16 discusses Israel disloyalty to their national family (v. 10), spiritual family (vv. 11-12) and marriage partners (vv. 13-16), evidenced by spiritual harlotry, mixed marriages with unbelieving partners, adultery and, finally, divorce.

In verses 11-12, Israelites are charged with unashamedly marrying women who worshiped other gods. Such religiously mixed marriages flew right in the face of warnings to the contrary (Ex 34:12-16; Num 25:1-3; Deut 7:3-4; 1 Kings 11:1-13). But there were more accusations: "Another thing you do" (v. 13). They had caused the Lord's altar to be flooded with such tears and mourning that the Lord refused to accept further sacrifices. The tears resulted from broken marriage vows to which the Lord was a party, being a witness at every wedding. Put very simply, God said, "I hate divorce" (v. 16).

Two key words dominate this text: The word *one* (which occurs four times in vv. 10, 15) and the word *breaking/broken faith* (which appears five times in vv. 10, 11, 14, 15, 16).

The identity of the "one" in verse 10 is not Abraham, your father (Is 51:2), as Jerome and Calvin thought, or the patriarch Jacob, whom Malachi did mention elsewhere very frequently (1:2; 2:12; 3:6). Instead, it is God who created Israel (Is 43:1). Thus those who have the same father should not be dealing so treacherously with each other.

But who is the "one" in verse 15? Again it is not Abraham (as if the sentence read: "Did not one, that is to say, Abraham, do so [take a pagan Egyptian named Hagar to wife]?" with the prophet conceding the point and replying, "Yes, he did!" But Abraham is never called the "one" nor could his conduct in "putting away" Hagar be the issue here, since the divorced wives in Malachi's context were covenant wives, not pagan wives.

The subject of verse 15 must be God, and "the one" must be the object of the sentence, not its subject. As such, the "one" would parallel the "one flesh" of Genesis 2:24, for returning to

God's original instructions would be a natural way to dispute covenant-breaking divorces. In a similar manner, our Lord referred to Genesis in Matthew 19:4-6: " 'Haven't you read,' he replied, 'that at the beginning the Creator "made them male and female," and said, "For this reason a man will leave his father and mother and be united to his wife, and the two will become one flesh"?' " (see also Mk 10:7-9).

Even though the Hebrew does not explicitly indicate that the first clause of Malachi 2:15 is an interrogative or that *he* refers to God, both possibilities fit the context, previous Scripture and normative Hebrew grammar and syntax observed in other passages.

The resulting thought would be as follows: Why did God make Adam and Eve only one flesh when he could have given to Adam many wives or to Eve many husbands? Certainly God had more than enough creative power to furnish multiple sex partners! So why only "one"? Because God was seeking a godly offspring, a process incompatible with multiple partners.

The two examples of faithlessness this passage raises are: divorce and being unequally married to unbelievers. Both violate God's holy law. Marriage's covenant status is seen in other Old Testament passages, such as Genesis 31:50; Proverbs 2:17; Ezekiel 16:8; and Hosea 1—2. Genesis 2:24 most clearly defines marriage: It consists of "leaving" one's parents and "cleaving" to one's wife. The leaving and cleaving go together and in that order. Marriage, then, is a public act (leaving), in order to establish a permanent relationship (cleaving), and is sexually consummated (becoming one flesh). Any violation of this covenant is a breach of promise made in the presence of God and each other.

So fundamental and inviolable is the union created by this marriage covenant that nothing less than a rupture in sexual fidelity can begin to affect its durability (note Mt 5:31-32; 19:3-12). That such a rift may lead to one of the two grounds for breaking the marriage covenant (1 Cor 7 treats the other one) is hinted at in Jeremiah 3:8, where God "gave faithless Israel her certificate of divorce and sent her away because of all her adulteries." In effect, God divorced Israel. But note the grounds!

Accordingly, the Bible is not silent, either on divorce or on the reasons it may be granted. But when God still says that he hates divorce, we gather how strongly he desires to see marriage covenants succeed.

The Mosaic legislation never encouraged, enjoined or approved of divorce in Deuteronomy 24:1-4. Instead, it merely prescribed certain procedures if and when divorce tragically took place. The main teaching of Deuteronomy 24:1-4 forbids a man to remarry his first wife after he had divorced her and either he or she had remarried in the meantime. Unfortunately, the Authorized Version (King James), the English Revised Version, The American Standard Version and some others have adopted a translation of Deuteronomy 24:1-4 that adds to the confusion. On their incorrect rendering, divorce is not just permitted or tolerated, it is commanded when some "uncleanness" is present!

The conditional *if* which begins in verse 1 of Deuteronomy 24 continues through verse 3 with the consequence of the conditional sentence coming in verse 4 (contrary to all the incorrect renderings noted above). No Old Testament law instituted divorce; Hebrew law simply tolerated the practice while condemning it theologically.

Those objecting that the absolute statement of Malachi 2:16 precludes all arguments for a biblically permissible divorce do not take Scripture holistically. God is certainly able to qualify his own teaching with further revelation in other contexts. For instance, in Romans 13:1-7 God states that citizens must obey the civil powers that be, yet he qualifies that absolute in Acts 5:29: Citizens should obey God rather than any sinful civil law.

God's hatred of divorce is further expressed in the statement,

"one who covers his garment with violence." The "garment" refers to the ancient custom of spreading a garment over a woman,
as Ruth asked Boaz to do to claim her as his wife (Ruth 3:9; see
also Deut 22:30; Ezek 16:8). Thus to cover one's bed with violence was to be unfaithful to the marital bed and one's nuptial
obligations. The symbol of wedded trust, much like our wedding
ring, became the agent of violence toward these wives.

Index